MW01109504

"…This book is not just for the hurting, it's for
everyone." Dr J. Melvyn Ming

A
WOUNDED
HEART

AND HOW TO HEAL IT

By: Ted Britain

PRESS

www.xulonpress.com

To order workbooks or to schedule a
seminar please use the following contacts:

Ted Britain

14707 B Road

Delta, Colorado 81416

Call: 970-985-8177

E-mail: Tedbritain@kaycee.net

On the Web: www.Tedbritainministries.com

WHAT OTHERS ARE SAYING ABOUT *A WOUNDED HEART AND HOW TO HEAL IT*:

"Very few of us will get through life without experiencing deep hurt of one kind or another. My friend Ted Britain wrote this book for you; to help you heal the wounds in your life. Take what he writes to your own heart."

George O. Wood

General Superintendent of

the Assemblies of God

"The purpose of my writing is to commend the book, *A Wounded Heart* by Ted Britain, to you. Anyone who takes the time to read and apply the insights in this excellent teaching will greatly enrich themselves, and will be better equipped to understand and help those who are struggling with mental and physical suffering. Every principle the author espoused is clearly based on Scripture. Furthermore, the testimonies of people delivered by applying the truth in this teaching add great value to the book. I commend *A Wounded Heart* to you."

Charles T. Crabtree

President, Zion Bible College

Former Assistant General Superintendent

of the Assemblies of God

"It is a privilege to write this brief word for my friend, Ted Britain, regarding his book, *A Wounded Heart*. As I read this teaching on forgiveness, I was struck with the practicality of the message. Well illustrated from a pastor's perspective, but also from the experience of a son with his father. In my fifty-plus years of ministry and of helping people, I have noted again and again the devastating effects of non-forgiveness and bitterness. These negative emotions can ruin a person's spiritual progress, as well as to cause physical problems that medicine cannot cure.

I commend this reading to you with the belief that many hurts will be healed and many lives strengthened. Pastor Britain has provided a wonderful tool for hurting people. Read it chapter-by-chapter. Do the work at the conclusion of each of those chapters. Why?

Because hateful people are hurting people; and bitter people are wounded people. These things can hang over our heads like a thick, dark cloud. May you find freedom through your response to the truths expounded in this volume."

Glen D. Cole

Pastor, Trinity Life Center,

Sacramento, CA

Pastor Emeritus, Capital Christian Center,

Sacramento, CA

Superintendent Emeritus, Northern

California/Nevada Assemblies of God

"As a cardiologist and previous member of Pastor Britain's church I strongly affirm both the messenger and the message of this book. Its Godly principles can free you from the disease consequences of unforgiveness."

Wayne Wright, M.D.

Cardiology

"In *A Wounded Heart*, author Ted Britain communicates vital principles in a clear, compelling fashion that connects with the reader. The power of the message goes beyond theory and demonstrates through stories told the change that can come to a person when they are healed of life's wounds through true forgiveness.

As a policy maker, I believe it is important to understand that actions taken by individuals that improve personal well being results

in more productive workers, stronger families, and healthier communities. That is the
subtle power and hopeful outcome of individuals applying these important concepts to
their lives."

Rep. Kenneth G. Summers
House of Representatives
State of Colorado

"*A Wounded Heart* deals with an issue
almost all of us will face. How to forgive
those who hurt us and get over the bitterness
that destroys our life. This book is not just for
the hurting, it's for everyone. I highly recom-
mend it to you."

Dr J. Melvyn Ming
Founding Partner of Leadership
Development Resources, LLC

"What a wonderful volume on such a relevant and critical subject. I love the format, particularly the discussion questions at the end of each chapter. This serves to bring the subject matter "home" to the reader and encourage personal application.

Forgiveness is a powerful tool afforded by God as an antidote to the blight of bitterness that affects so many of us, both inside and outside of the church. Proper application of this powerful tool will not only heal the individual who suffers from the side effects of bitterness, but individual healing will produce greater wholeness in the Body of Christ in turn. Ted Britain has done a commendable job of presenting time-tested Biblical solutions with clarity, relevance, and practicality."

Les Welk, Superintendent Northwest Ministry Network of the A/G

"We live in a world of people with wounded hearts, and unforgiving attitudes. They are the ones who suffer the most from their own malady. Ted Britain has endeavored to allow the Holy Spirit to guide his writing to bring healing and thereby restoration to those wounded hearts."

"Chapter two, alone, is worth the time spent reading and researching this fine work and chapter seven puts a beautiful crown on the entire message. The author is transparent with his own experiences and leads us, his readers, down a path to personal healing, deliverance, and victory. You will not only be blessed but will want to share it with others."

Derwood W. Dubose

Former District Superintendent

North Texas District A/G

TABLE OF CONTENTS

DEDICATION

A Wounded Heart and How to Heal It,
is dedicated to "LaDell" – my sweetheart
and wife of 44 years.
She is filled with mercy and
has more patience and forgiveness
than anyone I know.

It was through her encouragement that,
when not traveling, I finally sat down
at my computer this past summer and
undertook writing this book.

ACKNOWLEDGMENTS

I would also like to thank my friend, Hal Donaldson, Founder and President of Convoy of Hope. He encouraged me to begin writing. As the Senior Editor of the leading weekly Christian magazine, TPE, he published my first articles. He reviewed the first draft of this manuscript and encouraged me to publish it. Without his friendship and encouragement there would be no book. Thanks Hal!

FORWARD
By
Duane Buhler

I t is my pleasure to introduce to you my friend and colleague, Ted Britain whom I have known since 1988 when he moved to Twin Falls, Idaho, and was the successful Senior Pastor of a large and growing congregation.

As a counselor and Instructor of Advance Pastoral Counseling at the Masters level both in the United States and in Singapore, I can endorse his teaching from the standpoint of being Biblically accurate and for successful therapy.

Since Ted served on our Presbytery Board while I was the Superintendent of the Southern Idaho District, I have worked closely with him in various capacities on numerous occasions. The Presbytery dealt with delicate tensions between people, pastors and their boards or congregations, and Ted contributed to many successful solutions.

Ted was also very involved with our missionaries and their overseas ministry. Since the need for forgiveness is universal and forgiveness works in all cultures, his ministry overseas was highly effective in the area of forgiveness.

You will discover that Ted loves people and has a compassionate heart, which is balanced by an intensity to see people helped through forgiveness and achieve the best they can be in a joyous and productive life.

Duane Buhler, Nampa ID
Ordain minister and Pastor for 56 years
Pastor Emeritus Christian Faith Center, Nampa, Idaho
Northwest University, Kirkland, Washington
Board of Directors 1987 – present
Adjunct Faculty, Asia Theological Center for Evangelism and Missions

INTRODUCTION

"Resign your Church, sell your house, and take your wife back to Colorado to help her parents."

I t was a quiet voice deep within my spirit and the thought startled me. It was July of 2004 and I was in my study at the church where I was pastoring on the Monterey Peninsula. I had been putting a sermon together for the following Sunday when suddenly, out of the blue, I heard this voice that was so compelling it almost seemed to be audible.

What I heard was so foreign to what I was doing and thinking that it shocked me. "Lord," I said. "I can't resign my church and move to Colorado. What would I do? How would we be able to live?" I had no savings, no retirement funds, nothing.

"Go," He said, *"and I will show you."*

I argued with God through the rest of the summer and into the fall; trying to point out things that He might have overlooked. Namely, all the reasons we could not just *"leave our church and move back to Colorado."*

Where would we live? How would I be able to make a living and pay the bills? We had never been able to buy a house because we could never get enough together for a down payment. But, God had taken us out to the Monterey Peninsula, one of the highest housing markets in America, and we had been able to buy a house. It was nothing short of a miracle from God. However, since we had only been in it for a year and nine months, it would mean that we would have to pay the mortgage company a penalty if we sold the house.

In October, I was teaching our annual stewardship series; the theme of the series was "Trusting God." In the third week of the series, I was once again exhorting people to "trust God" when the Spirit of the Lord whispered to me, *"If you want your people to trust God, why don't you?"*

As I closed the service, I announced I would like to call a special board meeting for the next evening. I had preached myself under conviction and, on that Monday night, I told my board that effective the first of the year I would be resigning my position with the church and moving back to Colorado.

"What are you going to do pastor?" they asked.

I responded that I really did not know; and I am sure that some of them did not believe me. I would like to tell you that what I was doing was taking a great step of faith, but I suppose in reality it was just a small step of obedience.

The house sold for a profit the first week it was on the market, so on January 4, 2005, we were on our way.

After putting everything we owned (except our clothes) into storage and moving into the farmhouse with LaDell's parents, I did absolutely nothing for three months. And then I rested a while. Well, it's hard to do nothing; you never know when you're finished!

One Sunday morning, we were attending our home church and the pastor had scheduled a special speaker for that week. As he approached the pulpit, I felt my spirit open and the Lord began to speak to my heart.

I always carried a notebook with me so I could take notes while listening to others; and I began to write what I felt the Lord was saying to me. To this day I cannot tell you what the speaker said, but I can tell you what I felt the Lord said to me.

"It's time for you to go and speak in the churches," He said.

"What do you mean? What do you want me to say?"

"I want you to teach restoration, healing and forgiveness."

I thought about this for what seemed a long time. *"Healing, forgiveness, restoration . . . What did it all mean?"*

Then I remembered a series of messages I had taught back in 1995, when I was in Idaho; and again right after we had gone to Seaside, California in 2001. Once again I heard that voice in my spirit say, *"Our churches are full of hurting people and they don't know how to get rid of the hurt."*

Lord, if you want me to speak in churches, then you will have to open the doors; because I have been a pastor for thirty-three years and no one knows who I am except for the people in churches where we have pastored.

God has been faithful. Since that time in the spring of 2005, we have ministered in churches from California to Georgia, from

Oregon to West Virginia, and all over the state of Texas.

This book is a result of that ministry. I pray that it will be a blessing to you (the reader) and that, by God's grace, you will receive healing for your wounded heart.

CHAPTER ONE

RESPONDING WITH GOD'S GRACE

Her face brightened, her eyes began to sparkle, and she was grinning from ear to ear. As she got up from the altar and started toward me, her hands and arms were continuously moving in upward circles. "Oh! I just feel tons lighter," she said. "Oh! I just feel tons lighter!"

"Did you forgive someone tonight?" I asked.

"Yes. I did," she said.

"Who?" I asked.

"I forgave the four people who murdered my daughter," she said. "And I just feel tons lighter!"

Her answer stunned me. I really did not know how to react. To be perfectly honest, I am not sure I would be able to forgive someone for the murder of one of my sons or one of my grandchildren.

Only the supernatural grace of God moving in someone's life could help her to forgive such a grievous wound. Nevertheless, it produced a certainty in me that I had indeed heard God's voice when He told me to teach this series of messages on forgiveness.

In fact, five times in the past two years, someone has recounted to me his or her decision to forgive a family member's murderer. Furthermore, nearly every time I give the seminar, someone tells me of having forgiven a sexual molester for childhood abuse.

Just by living in this world, chances are that a parent, a sibling, a friend, a spouse, a teacher, a coach, or someone in a position of authority has hurt you.

If you go to church, you may be carrying wounds inflicted by a pastor, a deacon, a Sunday school teacher, or maybe by someone who just happened to sit beside you in the pew one day.

So, how do you handle life's wounds?

If you are like most people, you just try to forget. You push it to the back of your mind; or, you go to a therapist, dig a hole in your memory, and try to cover it up. The problem is, sooner or later, it will erupt like a volcano, all over you and everyone close to you.

Those around you who may have come to know you long *after* the initial wounding may react by thinking, *"Whoa! Where did that come from?!"*

There are really only two ways to deal with the wounds of life. Either we respond to them with the grace of God or we react with our natural tendencies.

"Looking diligently lest any man fail of the grace of God; lest any root of bitterness springing up trouble you, and thereby many be defiled."

Hebrews 12:15

Notice God is telling us to do something on a **conscious level**. It is not like breathing. It is not something we do automatically; rather, it is something that we are to make ourselves do: "*Look diligently*" so we will not fail of the grace of God. For if we "fail" to exercise the grace that God gives us, then a root of bitterness will spring up within our hearts.

When that root of bitterness springs up within us, then **every relationship** we have will be affected – one way or another. Obviously, the most affected relationship will be with the one toward whom we are bitter. That relationship is often cut off completely. Still, every other relationship we have - our relationship with our parents, our siblings, our spouses, our children, our friends and neighbors, our employers, or our employees - will be affected to some degree.

Let me illustrate:

Suppose something has happened. Someone has wounded you and you allow that wound to fester. Some time later, you walk into a store or public gathering place and see someone who looks like the one toward whom you are bitter. Instantly you think, *"I don't like that person."*

Why would you think that? You have never met the person in your life. Why would you automatically decide you do not like someone you have never met?

It is because they look like a person you do not like! Your relationship with this virtual stranger is already affected, as a consequence of the root of bitterness that has sprung up within your heart.

It all begins with a **wounded spirit.**

The wise man said in Proverbs 18:14 that the spirit of a man will sustain him in times of illness. But, *"a wounded spirit who can bear?"*

Something may be said or done to us, whether real or imagined . . . How *many of you know that people do not really have to say or do something to hurt us, we only have to think they did?* Either way, it can wound our spirit. We are then faced with a choice. Either we can respond with the grace of God or we *will* respond with our natural tendencies.

The grace of God has always been a great mystery to many people. What exactly *is* the grace of God?

When I was a boy in Sunday school, they taught us the definition of the grace of God. See if this sounds familiar: "The grace of God is His unmerited favor."

"So, what does that mean?" I asked my teacher.

"It means that God gives you something you don't deserve. He gives you something that you have not earned."

"Well, what does He give you?" I asked.

"Grace," my teacher replied.

"And what is grace?" I asked.

"Unmerited favor."

So round and round we went, until I finally found a definition for "grace" in the Scripture.

Paul tells us in Philippians 2:13, *"It is God which worketh in you both to will and to do of His good pleasure"*

To will means He gives us the desire and *to do* means He gives us the power. Therefore, Paul is telling us it is God Who gives us both the desire and the power to do His will.

So the "grace of God" is the "desire and the power to do His will."

Whatever it is we need, God gives us His grace to fulfill that need. He gives us both the desire and the power to walk in a way that is pleasing to Him.

Regarding *salvation*, for example, Scripture tells us that by grace we are saved through faith.

"For by grace are ye saved through faith: and that not of yourselves: it is the gift of God."

Ephesians 2:8

He is telling us that God has given us the desire for salvation and the power to exercise the faith He has given us; that we might be saved. Thus, it is *only* by the grace of God that we are saved.

41

Then what is the will of God for us when our spirit has been wounded? It is quite simple. The will of God for us, at that moment, is that we would forgive the one who wounded us.

But what happens if God gives us His grace (the desire and the power to do His will) and we fail to exercise that power?

If we "fail" to exercise the power He has given us, then we will respond with our natural tendencies.

When we respond with our natural tendencies, we **withdraw** our spirit from those who have wounded, hurt, or offended us.

When we withdraw our spirit, we become bitter. Our bitterness then causes us to become stubborn. Let's look for a moment at the progression of bitterness in the human heart.

"Bitter" is such an ugly word and it is something that none of us wants to claim. I have met very few people who would admit they are bitter. However, it is something that we can all readily see in others.

We do not realize that when we withdraw our spirit, a "root" of bitterness immediately springs up within our heart. Bitterness is not something that jumps on us full grown in all its ugliness. Rather, it begins as a tiny root within our hearts and thus we do not recognize it. Not only do we not recognize it, we refuse to admit that we could even *be* bitter.

We are like the proverbial frog that jumps into a pan of hot water and immediately jumps out. However, if he jumps into a pan of cold water and the heat is slowly turned up, he is cooked before he knows it!

So our bitterness *remains* unrecognized, and it causes us to become stubborn.

If you have teenage children or if *you* have been a teenager, you have probably experienced the following scenario:

You look down at the end of the dinner table during the evening meal and you see your teenager setting there with his arms crossed looking sad; or perhaps he has a fork in his hand and is absentmindedly pushing the peas into his mashed potatoes.

"What's the matter?" you ask.

"Nothing," he responds.

"No, really, what's the matter?"

"Nothing." And that is all you are going to get out of him. Why? Because he is *stubborn.*

Something happened that day. His spirit has been wounded. Perhaps it was wounded by you, a teacher, or a friend, and he has responded the way he has seen others respond - with their natural tendencies.

He has "failed of the grace of God," responded with his natural tendencies, and withdrawn his spirit. When he withdrew his spirit, he became bitter and his bitterness has caused him to become stubborn.

Stubbornness in turn leads to rebellion and rebellion is when the mind is placed under the control of Satan.

"For rebellion is as the sin of witch-craft, and stubbornness is as iniquity and Idolatry."

I Samuel 15:23

Stubbornness is simply the rejection of the proper God-ordained authority in our lives.

Rebellion, on the other hand, is the establishing of oneself as *the* authority.

The Scripture says that stubbornness is as idolatry. When a person is stubborn, he or she may still be looking to something or someone else as an authority. Whereas, rebellion is as witchcraft. In other words, it is the result of someone having established himself as *the* final authority in life. In reality, when we set ourselves up as the final authority in life, we have placed our minds under Satan's control.

In my seminar I ask the question, *"Who is the first person affected by our rebellion?"* The answer is usually *"me."* Some may think that the first one affected is God. However, the truth is that the first person(s) affected by our rebellion is *our children.*

"And Samuel said to Saul, thou hast done foolishly: thou hast not kept the commandment of the Lord thy God, which he commanded thee for now would the Lord have established thy kingdom upon Israel for ever. But now thy kingdom shall not continue."

I Samuel 13:13-14a

Here, Samuel is telling Saul that because he rebelled against the Lord's commandment, his son was not permitted to take his place as king of Israel. Had Saul walked in obedience to God, his son would have succeeded to the throne and his grandson after him, etc. *"But now,"* he said, *"thy kingdom shall not continue."*

Saul, for the time being, was still king. Jonathan was the first one affected by Saul's rebellion.

You see, when you rebel, your children will lose the Godly heritage they could have had if you had continued to walk in the grace of God.

As one who has pastored for thirty-three years, I can say I have seen it happen many times. The pastor, a deacon, or perhaps just a friend in the church hurts someone and, instead of responding with the grace of God and forgiveness, that person responds out of natural tendencies and withdraws his or her spirit.

Often when people who attend church withdraw their own spirit, they quit going to church, or they attend somewhere else. Many times this happens just as their children are entering their teenage years.

Later, mom and dad may forgive the one who hurt them, their wounds may then heal, and they return to their former church. But, at that point, their children are gone.

Why?

Because, when we rebel against the Lord's disciplines, we fail to learn spiritual insights and develop the character traits that God intended for us to learn and develop; therefore, we fail to pass these insights on to our children. How many of you understand that you cannot pass on something you yourself do not have? In sum:

1. In the first stage of rebellion, our children's future is affected.

2. In the second stage, as we continue to walk in rebellion, our own position is in jeopardy. Remember, Samuel told Saul, *"The kingdom is taken from you."*

3. In the third stage of rebellion, we submit to the enemy's control. Saul did not repent and he followed his natural inclination. He consulted a witch.

Wait a minute! *Why would I say it was natural for Saul to consult a witch?*

Doesn't the Bible say that God hand-picked Saul? Wasn't Saul a godly young man? Doesn't the Scripture say the Spirit of the Lord had come upon him and he prophesied? Yes! All these things are true; but now as Saul walks in rebellion, God said that rebellion is as "witchcraft," and when someone is into witchcraft what do they do? They consult witches.

4. In the forth stage of rebellion, we are destroyed. After Saul has placed his mind under Satan's control, he commits suicide.

The word of God tells us that Satan comes to *kill, steal,* and *destroy.*

Did you know that suicide is the second leading cause of death among teenagers? Car accidents are the leading cause of death among teenagers; and no one knows how many of these "accidents" may actually be suicides.

How do you suppose Satan encourages a young person living in America to commit suicide? It is hard to imagine that he can, since young people living in America have more opportunities and advantages than teenagers living anywhere else in the world.

Well, it is really quite simple. Satan arranges for their spiritual wounding, after which they follow the life patterns modeled for them by mom and dad, by teachers, or by peers. And they respond to life's wounds according to their natural tendencies.

These wounds may be emotional or physical; real or imagined. Regardless, when they reject the grace of God, their natural response is to withdraw their spirit and become embittered.

Bitterness causes one to become stubborn. Stubbornness leads to rebellion, and in the forth stage of rebellion one will commit suicide.

You can always spot a teenager in the third, or forth, stage of rebellion!

I remember seeing her come into the sanctuary. It was a Wednesday night and we were having a special service wherein we had invited the youth to join the adults in the main auditorium.

This particular young woman had accepted a friend's invitation to attend the youth service that night. As she entered, heads turned.

Her hair was done up in coal black spikes. Her eye shadow and lipstick were coal black. Her fingernail polish was black; she had tattoos all over her arms; and she was wearing a black T-shirt and tight black jeans. To top it all off, there were numerous piercing in her ears, eyebrows, nose, and lips. She was making a statement. She was anti-establishment.

That night it seemed the Spirit of God came into our service in a special way, and the church was filled with people seeking God. People were weeping and praying around the altar, down the aisles, even in the church foyer.

At 11:30 that evening, I was praying with people in the foyer when the main doors opened. It was a mother looking for her daughter. She said her daughter, who was grounded, had asked to be allowed to go to a youth service at the church; saying she would be home at 8:30 p.m.

When she described her daughter, I told her she was praying at the altar. At midnight, as I returned to the front of the church, I saw mother and daughter on their knees with their arms around each other, weeping and forgiving one another.

God, by His grace, had healed a hurt and reconciled a rebellious teenager with her mother.

Are all rebellious teenagers that easy to spot? Yes! They can be spotted by their dress, by their body language, and by their attitudes.

One fact our national media has not reported is that every school shooting here in America was perpetrated by individuals in the fourth stage of rebellion; who were heavily involved in witchcraft.

We must not lose sight of the fact that these young people had been wounded in their spirits.

SO HOW DO WE AVOID BEING WOUNDED IN LIFE?

How many of you know you cannot live life without being wounded? Most of us cannot make it through a day without some kind of wound. Therefore, we need to learn to respond to the wounds of life, with the grace of God.

Now, I have said all of that to say this:

NOTHING ANYONE DOES TO YOU CAN MAKE YOU BITTER!!!

I know people always want me to prove that statement. When we do seminar presentations on this material, we use a visual illustration that helps to prove the point, and I will try to describe it here in print.

I take an opaque glass of water from under the pulpit and ask for a volunteer to come forward to help. Handing them the glass of water, I usually walk to the other side of the altar area (to keep from getting wet), then ask them to "shake" the glass.

The reaction is always the same. They try to shake the glass *carefully* without spilling the water. At this point, I encourage them to, "Shake it harder. Oh, come on! Shake it real hard." Then, I might have to reassure them that I have already talked to the pastor or the janitor and it will be all right. So they shake it really hard and water goes everywhere.

I thank them, take the glass back, allow them to return to their seat, and then I ask, "How many of you think that 'shaking the glass' caused water to spill out of the glass?"

Most of the people respond by putting their hands up. Then I will pick on someone who raised a hand, "Would you please come up and help me?"

Next, I will take an identical, but empty, opaque glass from under the pulpit and give it to them, asking them to "shake it."

Of course, water does not come out of the glass no matter how hard they shake it. I remind the congregation that they said, "Shaking the glass would cause water to come out."

"Well, he's shaking the glass, why isn't water coming out?"

Someone always cries out, "Because the glass is empty."

"That's my point," I reply. "When someone hurts you, they do not put *bitterness* in your heart. They are just *shaking* you and that which is *already* in your heart comes out.

No one makes you bitter. No one makes you angry. People just shake you, and if there is bitterness or anger in your heart, it will come out. Whereas, if there is *grace* in your heart, and you do not *"fail of the grace of God,"* then grace will come out.

I can usually tell when there are people who are not convinced by this illustration. Perhaps you are one of them. *How would you like concrete proof? How about steel rein-forced concrete proof? Well then, how would you like Biblical proof?*

In Mark, chapter 7, verses 14-23, we read this account:

"Again Jesus called the crowd to him and said, "Listen to me; everyone, and

understand this. Nothing outside a man can make him unclean, by going into him. Rather, it is what comes out of a man that makes him unclean." After He had left the crowd and entered the house, his disciples asked him about this parable. "Are you so dull?" he asked. "Don't you see that nothing that enters a man from the outside can make him unclean? For it doesn't go into his heart but into his stomach, and then out of his body. (In saying this, Jesus declares all foods "clean.")..." (NIV)

Well . . . thank you brother Mark! By putting that parenthetical statement in, under the inspiration of the Holy Spirit, Mark has just given us permission to have bacon for breakfast.

He went on: "What comes out of a man is what makes him unclean. For from within, out of men's hearts, come evil thoughts, sexual immorality, theft, murder, adultery, greed, malice, deceit, lewdness, envy, slander, arrogance and folly. All these evils come from inside and make a man unclean." (NIV)

In this Scripture, the Lord tells us that feelings such as anger, bitterness, etc., are already in us; and when somebody shakes us, it just *reveals* what is already there.

So, how do we get rid of all these dark things in our hearts? I'm so glad you asked!

1. Step one: **HUMBLE** yourself.

I Peter 5:5 says:

"All of you, clothe yourselves with humility toward one another, because, God opposes the proud but gives grace to the humble." (NIV)

When I was a young pastor, I used to teach that God was just standing there with open arms receiving everyone that came to Him. However, that is not Scriptural. This verse in I Peter tells us there is a class of people whom God is actually pushing away from Himself.

If you try to approach God in your pride, He will push you away. *"God opposes the proud."* But if we will *humble* ourselves, God will give us His grace. (The desire and the power to do His will.) We cannot go to God on our own terms. We must go to Him on His terms. So, step number one, *"Humble yourself."*

2. Step two: **REPENT** of your bitterness.

A few years ago, I had the privilege of ministering on a Sunday morning at a district men's retreat. I felt the Lord had directed me to teach on the subject of forgiveness. As I closed the service, I encouraged the men to "humble themselves, repent of their bitterness," and "forgive the one who had offended them."

More than half of the 400 plus men in attendance at the service came forward for prayer. With such an overwhelming response,

I urged all the ministers who were not already at the altar to come and pray with someone. As I moved among the men, I begin to pray with an elderly gentleman. I'll call him Bill.

As soon as I started to pray with Bill, he began to justify his feelings of bitterness. The human mind is a powerful and wonderful thing. We seem to be able to rationalize anything and justify whatever we want to in any given moment.

"What would you do with a partner who cheated you out of forty thousand dollars?" he asked. Then he started to tell me the whole story. The more he got into it, the more emotional he became until finally, he was weeping.

"Wow," I thought. *"This is Sunday morning. As fresh as this wound is, he must*

have just found out about it on Friday; before
he came to the retreat."

"Bill," I said. "I don't need to hear all the
details; but tell me, when did this happen?"

"Forty years ago," he said.

"Forty years ago!" I responded. "And
you're still bitter about it?"

"Oh . . . I'm not bitter," he said.

"Listen, Bill," I said. "If this happened
forty years ago, you're still hurting, and you
get this upset whenever you think about it
– you are bitter."

The Spirit of God immediately convicted
Bill of his bitterness. He fell to his knees and
began to repent. Then I led him through the
final step that brought total healing for the
wound that had been festering and hurting
him for *forty* years.

3. Step three: **FORGIVE** the offender.

The third step toward healing for life's wounds is for us to *forgive* those who have hurt and offended us.

I was teaching the material in this book as a series for a church we were pastoring, and on the third Sunday of the series, a young lady came to the altar. I will call her Sarah. Sarah was in her early twenties and, in describing her, I can only say that she looked "hard." Her face looked hard; the way she did her hair made it look hard; and, when you shook her hand, her hands felt hard.

My wife knelt beside Sarah to pray for her and asked her why she was weeping.

"I need to forgive someone," she said. *"And I don't want to."*

"Who do you need to forgive?" my wife asked.

"My father and my uncle," she said.

"What did they do?"

The gentleness and love that Sarah felt from my wife caused her to open long-closed doors to her past and she talked about the hurts she had never told anyone.

"From the time I was five, until I was thirteen," she said, *"my father and my uncle sexually abused me!!"*

Even though she did not feel like it, Sarah prayed and forgave her father and her uncle. As she formed the words, *"Father, as an act of my will, I choose to forgive my father and my uncle,"* God brought healing to the hurts she had been harboring for nearly twenty years.

"Pastor Britain, are you condoning such vile action?" you may ask.

Absolutely not! The father and the uncle are in prison where they belong. However, Sarah needed to forgive them to obtain healing for her heart.

We need to understand there is a difference between *forgiveness* and *pardon*. Pardon means to take away all consequences for one's actions. We do not have the authority or the power to pardon; but we must always forgive.

If you were to go into that church today and try to find Sarah, based on my description of her, you would not find her. Sarah has gone through a complete transformation. Today, Sarah looks "soft."

Do you have a hurt that needs healing? Are you carrying a terrible wound from your past? Then join me and pray this prayer - right out loud.

"Father, I confess that I've been hurt. I humble myself before you. And I confess that I have been bitter. I repent of my bitterness. Now, as an act of my will, I choose to forgive _____."

You will notice that there is a blank space at the end of that prayer. That is where you can put the name of your offender.

When you are ready to pray that prayer in sincerity you will find it will bring healing to the wounds of life.

Rebecca (not her real name) experienced such healing after a Sunday morning service in the Spring of 2006.

I was in Nucla, a small town in Southwest Colorado. If you travel West, Northwest on highway 141, make a right turn on Colorado

97 at Naturita, go up the hill, and drive about five miles North (being careful to watch for deer on the highway), you will be in Nucla. On the North edge of town, there is a sign that says, "Highway ends here." You do not go through Nucla when traveling anywhere. If you go to Nucla, it would mean you traveled there on purpose.

I went to Nucla on purpose. Pastor Gangwish had asked me to come and teach the seminar on forgiveness. During the altar service, while I was leading those who had responded to forgive those who had offended them, I noticed a young lady weeping almost uncontrollably.

That evening, a few minutes before the service was to begin, I asked the pastor if he had noticed the young lady weeping at the altar after the morning service, and whether he knew where she was?

"Yes," he said, "her name is Rebecca (not her real name), and she is sitting right over there on the front row." I looked, but I did not recognize her. Her whole countenance had changed. She looked entirely different.

I asked the pastor, "What is her story. Why was she weeping like that?" He said she had moved to Nucla from the New England area several years earlier. She had two young boys. One was 15 years old and the other about 10 years old.

"Fifteen years ago, while living in New England," he said, "and just before her son was born, a man raped and killed her two year old daughter."

At the close of the evening service, Rebecca came up to me and said, "Pastor

Britain, it is absolutely God's timing that you were here, *this week*."

"What do you mean?" I asked, somewhat bewildered. "What's so special about, *this* week?"

"Well, next week I have to move back to New England and I have been dreading it. But now," she said, "I can go."

I do not understand how such horrific sins of that nature can be forgiven. But I do know that the grace of God is sufficient. And I could see in her eyes that her heart and soul were receiving a healing of her wounds.

A WORD OF CAUTION . . .

If you have just prayed and forgiven someone, do not - I repeat - *do not*, go to or call that person and say something like, "Hey, I have forgiven you."

He or she might ask, "For what?"

You do not have to talk to the one you have forgiven. That is between you and God.

There is one exception to this rule. If someone who has wounded or offended you came to you and *asked* for your forgiveness and you previously refused them, then you need to go immediately and tell them that you have now forgiven them.

CHAPTER ONE QUESTIONS

When we are wounded or hurt, what choices do we have?

1_____

_____

_____

2_____

_____

_____

Discuss "the grace of God." Give Scripture reference.

_____

_____

_____

_____

_____

_____

What happens when we *"fail of the grace of God"*? Give Scripture references.

_____

_____

_____

_____

_____

When we respond with our natural tendencies, we _____ our spirit.

When we _____ our spirit, we become _____.

Discuss the progression of bitterness.

_____

_____

_____

_____

What happens in the fourth stage of rebellion?

_____

_____

_____

_____

How do we avoid being wounded in life?

_____

_____

_____

_____

Do people make us bitter or angry? Give Scripture reference.

_____

_____

_____

_____

How do we get rid of the bitterness and anger that is in our hearts?

1_____

_____

_____

2_____

_____

_____

3_____

_____

_____

When should you contact someone to tell him that you have forgiven him?

_____

_____

_____

_____

_____

CHAPTER TWO

THE UNFORGIVING HEART

D o you have one person in your family who is always committing the same offense, over and over, and you're wondering how many times you should forgive them?

Join the club! Peter was a charter member of that club. Fortunately for us, he asked our greatest Biblical authority that question and received the definitive answer.

"Then came Peter to him, and said, Lord, how oft shall my brother sin against me, and I forgive him? Till seven times? Jesus saith unto him, I say not unto thee, until seven times: but, until seventy times seven."

Matthew 18:21-22

Seventy times seven; when I was in school that equaled 490 times. Is Jesus saying that we are to keep count and on the 491st time we no longer need to forgive? No, I don't think so.

I believe that Jesus is using hyperbole here, to show that we are to forgive a person as many times as they need to be forgiven.

It was Jewish tradition that you were to forgive a person "seven" times. I do not know if Peter had already forgiven someone seven times and was wondering if he should forgive them the eighth time or not. I do know that here in our American culture if we forgive a person twice, we feel like we qualify for sainthood.

However, Jesus is telling us that as often as people need forgiveness, we need to forgive them.

When Jesus said to forgive *"seventy times seven,"* I believe that He was extremely aware of the mental, emotional, physical, and spiritual consequences of nursing old wounds, and holding bitterness in our hearts.

That is what I want to talk about in this chapter: "The consequences of holding onto bitterness and unforgiveness."

I. There will be PHYSICAL consequences.

According to a recent article posted on MedicineNet.com, Dr. Sternburg is quoted saying, *"Chronic stress is associated with mental and emotional conditions such as depression and anxiety."* In the same and other articles posted on the website, *unforgiveness* is associated with "chronic stress."

Thus numerous medical doctors agree that bitterness and unforgiveness will cause many different kinds of stress hormone related diseases; including those affecting our immune system.

Our bitterness produces special hormones from the pituitary, adrenal, thyroid and other glands. Doctors know excesses of these hormones will cause diseases in many parts of our bodies.

Now, let's communicate. Do not read this and go away saying, "Pastor Britain said, I have high blood pressure, etc., because I'm bitter." That might be true, but there are *other causes* for those diseases as well.

Ladies, did you know that holding bitterness in your heart will cause *wrinkles*?

Refusing to forgive others will result in physical fatigue and loss of sleep. You might try to hide your resentments, but very soon they become etched into your eyes and facial muscles as a permanent reflection of your inward feelings.

I am told that every issue of a woman's magazine gives beauty tips. Well ladies, let me give you the greatest beauty tip of all time.

This is one you will not find in magazines, at the checkout lines in your local Wal-Mart.

It is found in I Peter 3:3-5:

"Whose adorning let it not be that outward adorning of plaiting the hair, and of wearing of gold, or of putting on of apparel"

Ok, let me interrupt for just a moment. This verse has probably been one of the most misunderstood and misinterpreted verses in the Bible.

Whole movements have been based on a false interpretation of I Peter, chapter 3; and thousands of sermons have been directed at women, telling them that they could not wear make-up, have a "fancy" hair-do, or wear jewelry.

I have never been able to understand how people can form doctrine on only half a verse of Scripture. If you are going to ban a fancy hair-do, make-up, and jewelry based on the King James Version of I Peter 3:3, then go ahead and ban the rest of the verse. It also says, *"and the putting on of apparel."*

Obviously, Peter is not saying that women should not wear make-up, have nice hair, jewelry, and designer clothing. He is saying that those things are not the "source" of their beauty.

He continues in verses 4-5:

"But let it be the hidden man of the heart, in that which is not corruptible, even the ornament of a meek and quiet spirit. Which is in the sight of God of great price. For after this manner in

85

the old time the holy women also, who trusted in god, adorned themselves."

That is quoting from the King James translation. Let me read it to you in the New International Version:

*"Your beauty should not come from outward adornment, such as braided hair and the wearing of gold jewelry and fine clothes. Instead, it should be that of your inner self, the unfading beauty of a gentle and quiet spirit, which is of great worth in God's sight. For this is the way the holy women of the past who put their hope in God used to **make themselves beautiful**."*

Here we clearly see that Peter is saying true beauty comes from within, from a *"gentle and quiet spirit."* Ladies, you cannot project beauty from your face while your heart is in turmoil with bitterness.

As a speaker, I have always been at a disadvantage. I could never tell "mother-in-law" jokes. My mother-in-law is a wonderful woman. How can I describe her? Silver hair, very elegant, and because she does not always eat right, a little on the thin side; still living alone and taking care of herself. Her hands are gnarled with arthritis and 86 years of hard farm work.

Yet, when people see her, they say, "What a beautiful lady." I have never met anyone with a gentler or quieter spirit than my mother-in-law.

Holding bitterness in our hearts will affect the health of our bones.

Leviticus 17:11 tells us that the life of the flesh is in the blood. But the factory for the blood is the marrow of our bones.

The health of our bones, therefore, determines the health of our bodies. Bitterness will have a direct and devastating effect upon our bones.

Psalm 32:3 (NIV)

"When I kept silent, my bones wasted away through my groaning all day long."

Proverbs 15:30 (NIV)

"A cheerful look brings joy to the heart, and good news gives health to the bones."

Proverbs 17:22 (NIV)

"A cheerful heart is good medicine, but a crushed spirit dries up the bones."

Another translation might read, *"A wounded spirit dries up the bones."*

Proverbs 14:30 (NIV)

"A heart at peace gives life to the body, but envy rots the bones."

Proverbs 12:4 (NIV)

"A wife of noble character is her husband's crown, but a disgraceful wife is like decay in his bones."

On a Sunday night in November 2007, I had just finished teaching a message on this subject of our bones, when a couple (I suppose in their mid-thirties) came up to me in the foyer and asked to talk. I will call them Jessica and Dan.

Dan was encouraging Jessica to "go ahead" and share her testimony with me.

"This morning," she said, "when you called us to the front to pray that prayer of forgiveness, I came with the others. At the close of the prayer when you said, 'There's a blank there, now you put in the name of the one you are forgiving,' I had a bunch of names to put there. From the time I was five years old, and for a number of years, several people in my family sexually abused me on a regular basis. When I was nine years old, I was lying on the living room floor when my uncle came into the room and fell on me, crushing all my ribs."

Jessica continued, "When I was sixteen, my family took me into the hospital for reconstructive surgery." As her hands circled and indicated her rib area, she said, "My sternum is my own but most of the rest of me is plastic."

"Since that day," she said, "I have been in pain every waking hour, seven days a week, for over fifteen years. The doctors have taken me back and done x-rays and MRIs and told me that everything was okay, but I was still in pain."

With tears of joy streaming down her cheeks, Jessica continued. "But this morning, after I prayed and forgave those who abused me, I suddenly noticed that I wasn't hurting. You had dismissed us from the altar, we had gone back to our seats, and I told Dan I was not hurting. I have not hurt all afternoon," she said. "And I'm not hurting now."

She continued, "All afternoon I wondered how this could be? And then tonight you taught about how bitterness can affect our bones."

"Apparently," she said, "even *plastic* ones!"

The next morning Jessica went to the church office and gave her testimony to her pastor. Six months later, when I personally spoke to her pastor, he told me that she was still pain free.

God is able to heal life's wounds instantly when we do what He has asked us to do, and choose to forgive those who hurt us.

In addition to the physical consequences for harboring bitterness . . .

II. There will be EMOTIONAL Consequences.

Doctors tell us that between 60-70 percent of all people in the hospital are sick from psychosomatic diseases.

Now, let's communicate clearly again. I did not say they just think they are sick. They really are sick. It is just that their sickness is a consequence of their emotional state.

Depression is one of the most significant consequences of refusing to forgive the people who hurt us.

It requires emotional energy to maintain a grudge. We all know that we become weary when our physical energy is exhausted; and it is just as true that we become depressed when our emotional energy is exhausted.

Besides that, bitterness and resentment will create an "emotional focus" toward the person who wounded us. This emotional focus is the main reason we become just like the one we resent. I made this statement to a young man once and he reacted in a very startled manner.

"What did you say?" he asked. "I'm nothing like my father; I don't do the things that he did. He was a womanizer and an alcoholic. I don't drink and I have never been unfaithful to my wife."

"And yet," I said, "Your wife, says that you are just like him. Not in the things you do, but in your attitudes."

You see, the more we focus on the offender's actions toward us, the more we resemble their basic attitudes - which were the cause of those actions.

So, if we hold bitterness and unforgiveness in our hearts, we will have physical problems, emotional problems, and . . .

III. There will be MENTAL consequences.

In his book *None of These Diseases*, S.I. McMillen illustrates the mental consequences of holding resentments by quoting a medical doctor, as follows:

"The moment I start hating a man, I become his slave. I can't enjoy my work any more because he controls my thoughts. My resentments produce too many stress hormones in my body, and I become fatigued after only a few hours of work. The work I formerly enjoyed is now drudgery. Even vacations cease to give me pleasure. I can't escape his tyrannical grasp on my mind. When the waiter serves me porterhouse steak, it might as well be stale bread and water. My teeth chew the food, and I swallow it, but the man I hate will not permit me to enjoy its taste."

Do you suppose this was the reason Solomon wrote in Proverbs 15:17 (NIV):

"Better a meal of vegetables where there is love than a fattened calf with hatred."

The wise man is simply saying. "You're better off having a salad with love, than a choice piece of veal with bitterness."

Finally . . .

IV. There will be SPIRITUAL consequences to harboring bitterness.

I am going to make a statement that may shock you. **If you are bitter, you cannot love God!**

No, this statement did not originate with me. John said it first in I John 4:20-21 NIV:

*"If anyone says, 'I love God,' yet hates his brother, he is a liar. For anyone who does not Love his brother, whom he has seen, **cannot** love God, Whom he has not seen."*

Wow, does anyone have a different translation?

This is very plain language, so we try to soften it by changing the name.

I don't hate him, I'm just **bitter**. Or,

I'm not bitter, I just **resent** him. Or,

Here's the one I always get,

"I'm not resentful,

I'm just **hurt**."

You need to understand:

Hurt is the H word for resentment.

Resentment is the R word for bitterness.

Bitterness is the B word for hate, and

Hate is the motive for,

Murder.

Hiding bitterness and unforgiveness in our hearts will also cause us to doubt our salvation.

As it turned out, that was Nellie's problem.

We had just become the pastors of a church in Twin Falls, Idaho, and I was in my office at 8:00 o'clock on a Monday morning. I heard the intercom click. "Pastor, Nellie Dickerson is here and wants to see you."

"Who is Nellie Dickerson?" I asked.

"I don't know," my secretary replied, "*but she said that you were her last hope.*"

My first thought was, *"If I'm her last hope, she doesn't have any hope."* Then my brain raced, trying to place who Nellie was. Having only been the pastor for three weeks at that point, my mind was filled with new names and faces.

After just a few moments, my secretary ushered her into the office. Nellie was a thin, elegant, 81-year-old lady. She was in unusually good health and walked with a steady gait, full of determination and purpose; but there seemed to be an air of sadness about her.

After the usual greetings, we sat down and I asked her what I could do for her.

"Pastor," she said, "I don't know if I'm saved! If a person is saved, shouldn't they feel something? I don't feel anything! If a person is saved, shouldn't they like other people? *I don't like people!* What can I do?"

Her question caught me a little off guard. I had never had anyone be quite that direct with me before. Trying to buy time so I could think of what to do, I said, "Nellie, why don't you tell me a little about yourself?"

Well, that was all it took. For the next two hours, I listened as she told me all about herself and her daughter.

Her daughter had MS and, toward the end of her life, Nellie quit her job as a legal secretary to take care of her daughter full time. She told me how her daughter moved to Denver, started going to church, was saved, but when she could no longer live alone, she came home to her mother. At that point, the two of them started to attend the church I was now pastoring.

Her daughter had died about a year before we came to Twin Falls, but Nellie had continued to attend services. Now in recent months she had begun to question her salvation.

I did not know what else to do, so I opened my Bible and began to show her the Scripture in Romans, which we often refer to as the "Roman road." After reading the Scripture about salvation, I knelt beside her chair and led her in the sinner's prayer.

When I finished she looked up at me and said, "I don't feel any different!"

I was about to respond with the old evangelical cliché, *"We don't walk by feelings. We walk by faith. Just believe the Word and tell the devil that you're trusting in Jesus and the feelings will come."* However, the Spirit of God checked me.

At this point, my mind went blank. I did not have a clue what to say to her. Then it was just as though the Spirit of the Lord took over and I heard myself saying something that I had not thought.

How many of you know it is dangerous to speak before you think?

Yet here I was, asking a question that had never crossed my mind before I spoke. "Nellie," I asked. "Were you ever married?" I will never forget her answer.

In a stern voice this petite and gentle little woman shook her finger at me and said, "*I told you I had a daughter!*"

I supposed she was saying, "*In my day you didn't have children unless you were married.*"

Again, I caught myself saying something that I had not previously thought.

"Yes, I know," I said. "You talked about you and your daughter for over two hours, but you never mentioned your husband."

When I said the word "husband," it seemed almost as if a dark cloud formed over her head and she began to tell me about her husband and her father - who had both been alcoholics and had been physically and emotionally abusive.

As she talked, emotion almost over-whelmed her as though she were going through the hurt all over again. The hurt seemed so fresh that I assumed her husband had knocked her around before she came to my office that morning.

I could feel anger rising up within me. I just wanted to give that guy a little taste of his own medicine. I was in my mid-forties at the time and in pretty good shape. At 210 pounds, I figured I could take a man in his eighties. However, with just a few more questions, I discovered her husband had been dead for seven years.

Seven years. He had been dead for seven years and the mere mention of the word "husband" could still open old wounds and put her into an emotional tailspin.

It was then the Spirit of the Lord once again took the lead and I asked her if she had a concordance in her Bible.

"Yes," she said, "I do."

"Do you know how to use it?" I asked.

"I do," she replied.

"Well, I know you know how to read," I said. "Because you told me you were a legal secretary."

"So here's what I want you to do, I want you to look up the word "forgive," "forgiveness," or any derivative of those words and write down all the references for me. When you get that done, call and we'll make another appointment."

That was Monday. On Wednesday morning, Nellie was back in my office.

What a change. Instead of the air of sadness and the cloud of gloom, there was a smile enveloping her face, brightness in her eyes, and a new assurance of her salvation.

"Nellie," I said. "What did you find out?"

"I found out," she said, "that if I didn't forgive my husband, God could not forgive me."

"Nellie, where in the world did you read something like that?" I asked.

"In Matthew, chapter six," she replied.

*"Our Father which art in heaven, Hallowed be thy name. Thy kingdom come. Thy will be done in earth, as it is in heaven. Give us this day our daily bread. And **forgive us our debts, as we forgive our debtors**."*

Let me interpret that last line for you.

We are to pray, *"Father, I want you to forgive my sins exactly the same way that I forgive those that hurt and offend me."*

"Well," you say, "that's a little over the top."

"Ok, let's see how Jesus interprets it." In chapter six, verses 14-15, He said:

*"For if ye forgive men their trespasses, your heavenly Father will also forgive you: But if ye forgive not men their trespasses, **neither will** your Father forgive your trespasses."*

"And Nellie, did you forgive your husband?" I asked. After seeing the smile on her face, I did not need to ask that question; but just for the record, I did.

"Oh yes," she said. "And it feels so good not to be carrying that burden around anymore."

Since that day I have witnessed the same miraculous instantaneous change in many people who choose, as an act of their will, to forgive someone in their past who has offended them.

From that day until she went to be with her Lord at the age of 93, I never saw Nellie without that big smile. During the Spring and Summer, the altar always had fresh flowers from Nellie's garden; and she started giving fresh vegetables from her garden to her neighbors because, as she said, *"I just love people."*

Finally, as I close this chapter, let me remind you that if you hold bitterness and unforgiveness in your heart, it will surely multiply.

Deuteronomy 5:9 (NIV) says:

"For I the Lord your God am a jealous God, punishing the children for the sin of the fathers to the third and fourth generation of those who hate me."

One translation says, "To the third and fourth generation of those who hold hatred within their hearts."

If you think you can keep those grudges, hold unforgiveness in your heart, and not suffer the physical, emotional, mental, and spiritual consequences we have been talking about, think again!

During the first year that we were in Twin Falls, Idaho, a local Christian radio station would broadcast our Sunday morning service live. The listening area included most of Idaho, Southwestern Montana, Western Wyoming, and Northern Utah and Nevada.

The first time I ever taught this series on forgiveness, I started on a Sunday morning and the message included much of what is included in the first chapter of this book.

At Wednesday evening Bible study, I taught the subject of this chapter on the consequences of bitterness.

Then, that Thursday morning, I was opening my mail and found a letter; six hand-written pages from an elderly lady in Southwestern Montana.

She told me how the teaching broadcast on Sunday had affected her; and, for the first time in her life, she was free from bitterness. She talked about how both she and her husband had become bitter as children and had carried that bitterness all their lives.

She mentioned all the physical, emotional, mental, and spiritual problems that their family (she and her husband, her children and her grandchildren) had gone through. And how she wished she had heard this teaching earlier in life.

You would have thought that I had taken my outline for teaching "The Consequences of Holding Bitterness in Your Heart" from her letter. Yet, I had not received her letter until the day after I taught that lesson; and she had not heard that lesson, because I taught it on a Wednesday night. Sunday morning was the only time our services were broadcast.

Folks, if there is bitterness in our hearts, we need to get rid of it. And the only way to get rid of it is to forgive. You might say, *"I don't feel like forgiving, I don't want them to get away with what they did."* Well, read on. That is what the next couple of chapters are about: "Godly Character" and "How to Develop a Forgiving Heart."

CHAPTER TWO QUESTIONS

How often should we forgive someone? Give Scripture reference.

_____

_____

_____

_____

_____

Discuss the consequences of holding bitterness and unforgiveness in your heart.

1_____

_____

_____

2_____

_____

_____

3_____

_____

4 _____

Discuss, "The Lord's Prayer."

How does unforgiveness multiply? Give Scripture reference.

_____

_____

_____

_____

_____

_____

_____

_____

CHAPTER THREE

DEVELOPING GODLY CHARACTER

R omans 8:28 is a verse we all know by heart. Let's see if we can quote it:

*"And we know that **most** things work together for good to them that love God . . ."*

I can almost hear some of you saying, "No, that's not right."

Well, let's try it again. *"And we know that* **the overwhelming majority** *of things work together for good..."*

"No?" Let's try it one more time.

"And we know that **all** *things ...* (Everybody say, "**all**.") *"all things work together for good to them that love God, to them who are the called according to his purpose."* I think we got it right that time.

There is just one problem with that verse. We don't believe it!

Oh, we believe it when everything is going our way. But, how about when things are going wrong? How about when our world is falling apart? How about when someone offends, hurts, or abuses us? How about when tragedy strikes our family?

We closed the last chapter by quoting Jesus when He said, *"If you do not forgive men their sins, your Father will not forgive your sins."*

Forgiveness deals with the response of our will toward our offender. Pardon deals with the consequences of their offense. We do not have the authority to "pardon" the offender, but we must forgive.

Forgiveness will make it possible for us to have the same openness toward them after they offend us as we had before they offended us.

We need to step back a moment and look at forgiveness from God's point of view.

1. **Forgiveness involves a positive attitude toward the offense, rather than a negative attitude toward the offender**. If our initial focus after being offended is on the person who

offended us, it will be very difficult for us not to become bitter.

But, if we first focus on the offense and forget for the moment who it was that offended us, we will be more able to view the offense as being part of our personal character development.

If you have made a profession of faith in Jesus Christ as your Savior then, when you trusted Him, you were instantly cleansed of your sins. Now God will spend the rest of your life helping you to develop Godly character traits.

While we were pastoring in Nebraska, I made a statement one night that really offended Rachel (not her real name).

In retrospect, knowing what I know about her now, I can fully understand why she was so upset.

Rachel was a young, single mother of three small children and her life was in the pits. She had just gone through a very ugly and hurtful divorce and was working several jobs just trying to keep her family together. In addition, she was in a custody battle for her children. In short, her world was falling apart and the pain and hurt was almost more than she could stand.

What offended her was that I said, "What happens to you in life is not important. What's important is how you respond to what happens to you."

When I made that statement, it ticked her off!

"How dare he?" She thought. "He doesn't know me, and He doesn't have a clue what's happening in my life, how dare he tell me what's happening to me is not important?"

She was very offended by the statement and responded with her natural tendencies. Withdrawing her spirit, she quit coming to church.

Some months later, she came back to church. Approaching me, she asked if we could talk. *"Pastor Britain, do you remember some months ago making the statement, 'What happens to us in life is not important. What's important is how we respond to what happens to us'?"*

"Yes," I said. *"I made that statement."*

"Well, when you said that, it made me very angry and I quit coming to church. But that night when I went to bed, I could not get to sleep. All night I kept thinking, *'It's not important what happens to me, what's important is how I respond to what happens to me.'"*

"That phrase just kept going over and over in my mind."

She said when she went to work the next day she could not concentrate, because she could not get that phrase out of her head.

Her boss came in and "chewed her out," and she said all she could think was, *"It's not important what's happening to me, what's important is how I respond to what's happening to me."*

Do you remember what I said earlier, "Bitterness will cause an emotional focus?"

Well, Rachel was focused on that phrase and she said, "Pastor, I discovered that the way I respond to what is happening in my life is what is most important. Because when I changed my attitude, God begin to change my circumstances. And Pastor, don't ever quit teaching that."

You see, as a result of being offended, our attitude becomes the important issue, because it will point out the *lack* of character qualities that God is trying to help us build in our lives.

"What character qualities?" you may ask. Well, God points out several in Matthew, chapter 5:

Character qualities like humility, repentance, meekness, spiritual hunger, mercy, purity, peacemaking, endurance in persecution, etc.

Let me ask you a question. *"How can you develop, endurance in persecution, unless you're being persecuted?"*

Then there are the character qualities that we call the "fruit of the Spirit," found in Galatians 5:22. This is the fruit the Holy Spirit wants to produce in your life: love, joy, peace, patience, gentleness, goodness, faith, meekness, and self-control.

Have you ever prayed for patience?

Do you know how the Scripture tells us we will develop patience?

The Scripture in Romans, chapter 5, verse 3 says, *"Tribulation worketh patience."*

I looked up the word "tribulation" in Strong's Concordance. It means, "severe problems or trials." So if the Lord wanted to help you develop patience, He would allow severe problems or trials to come into your life.

"And we know that all things work together for good."

I also looked up the definition of the word "patience." I found there were two words in the Greek that we translate as "patience" in English. One of those words means "patience with circumstances," the other means "patience with people."

I do pretty well with the first one. If circumstances are beyond my control, I can usually roll with the punches. Whereas, circumstances beyond her control drives my wife up the proverbial wall.

However, my wife is very patient with people. I, on the other hand, think, that after three or four times, people ought to "get it" (whatever *it* may be). When they don't, I get a little exasperated.

God is always trying to help me to learn, "patience with people."

You might not want to play golf with me. I think the Lord always sees to it that the slowest foursome on the course is right in front of me, and they will not let me play through. The one that really gets me is when there are two cars driving side by side on the interstate; both of them five miles per hour below the speed limit.

I just want to shout, *"Get a clue! Get over and let those of us who have somewhere to go get on with it."*

Now, which word do you think God uses the most in the New Testament? That's right - patience with people. So, if the Lord wanted to help you develop patience with people, He would send people into your life that just "irritate the tar" out of you.

Do you have someone in your life that irritates you? God is using it for your good.

2. Forgiveness not only involves a positive attitude toward the offense, but it **views the offense as a tool in the hands of God.**

In II Samuel, chapter 16, David could have become bitter toward Shimei who tried to humiliate David by publicly cursing him. David's general said, "David, let me go over and lop that turkey's head off?"

But David viewed him simply as an agent of God. He told the general, *"No, leave him alone, the Lord hath bidden him to curse me."*

Jesus could have become bitter toward those who beat and nailed him to the cross, but He looked upon them as carrying out God's purpose for His life. Because of this, He was able to say, **"Father forgive them."**

3. Forgiveness recognizes that **bitterness is assuming a right we do not have. Only God has the right to punish.**

"Do not take revenge my friends, but leave room for God's wrath, for it is written: "It is mine to avenge; I will repay," says the Lord."

Romans 12:19 NIV

We have a problem with this verse, too. Again, our problem is, we don't believe it. Many people believe that God needs their help to extract revenge.

May I say something here? If your god needs your help in extracting revenge, then you need to get a bigger god.

God does not need or want our help; but a response of bitterness is an instinctive means of revenge toward the one who has offended us. Most of us are prone to withdraw our spirit and use silence toward the offender as a means of punishing that person.

But God's word tells us not to do that. We are to *"leave room for God's wrath."* That means we are to leave it alone and let God handle it.

Many of us are like Jonah, we just don't believe that God will punish our enemy or we don't really believe He can. Either way, we don't want God to let them "off the hook."

When God had mercy on Nineveh and spared them, Jonah went out and threw a "hissie fit."

Stomping around on the ground and shaking his fist in the air, Jonah shouted at God, "I knew it, I knew it! I knew you were going to forgive them."

And that's how we often feel. If anyone is going to be punished, *we* will have to do it. God certainly is not going to do it. At least, not soon enough for us.

Nevertheless, God's word is very clear:

"Do not repay anyone evil for evil. Be careful to do what is right in the eyes of everybody, If it is possible, as far as it depends on you, live at peace with everyone. Do not take revenge, my friends, but leave room for God's wrath, for it is written: "It is mine to avenge; I will repay," says the Lord. On the contrary: "If your enemy is hungry, feed him; if he is thirsty, give him something to drink. In doing this, you will heap burning coals on his head."

Romans 12:17-20 NIV

He also tells us we are to:

"Do good to them that hate you, and pray for them which despitefully use you, and persecute you."

Matthew 5:44

So how do we pray for them? Do we pray for them the way David prayed for his enemies in the Psalms?

"God, Kill'em!!!"

I don't think that's what Jesus had in mind. Although we feel that way, most of us wouldn't verbalize it. No, we are much more spiritual than that. What we pray is, "God, convert'em."

What we really mean when we pray for our enemies that way is, *"God make them just like me, so they will think like I think, and come to see that I was right all along."*

I believe that the way we should really pray for our enemies is to pray, *"God, bless them. Bless their home, bless their business, bless their family; Lord, just bless their socks off."*

In praying like that, it would not be long before we would genuinely start to care for them.

4. To forgive someone means we will **cooperate** with God in the life of that one who offended us.

When people intentionally offend you, you can be sure they will be watching to see what kind of response they get. At that point, you have an opportunity to demonstrate the love and forgiveness of God to them.

As they see your love for them, they will be able to understand the same love that God has toward them in spite of their offenses toward God.

When people unintentionally offend you, it indicates that the offender has personal deficiencies, which they themselves may not fully understand.

In that case, your continued love toward them will provide the opportunity for God to work in their lives.

Forgiveness means that we could use the hurts of others as the foundation for demonstrating Christ's love back to them. I am sure you have heard the saying "hurting people hurt people."

So, when someone hurts you, one of your first thoughts should be, *"Oh my, that person must be hurting."*

Let's take a look at these verses in Matthew 18 (NIV):

"Therefore, the kingdom of heaven is like a king who wanted to settle accounts with his servants. As he began the settlement, a man who owed him ten thousand talents was brought to him."

Matthew 18:23-24

I have seen "ten thousand talents" translated as being anywhere from two million to twenty million dollars, depending on the "weight of a talent" and the price of gold.

Do any of you owe someone two million dollars? If you do, could you pay them today?

If you can, I would like to talk with you about supporting a ministry!

> *"Since he was not able to pay, the master ordered that he and his wife and his children and all that he had be sold to repay the debt. The servant fell on his knees before him, be patient with me' he begged, 'and I will pay back everything'. The servant's master took pity on him, canceled the debt and let him go."*
>
> Matthew 18:25-27

Did you see that? He didn't just give the servant more time to pay, he canceled the debt.

"But when that servant went out, he found one of his fellow servants who owed him a hundred denarii . . ."

Matthew 18:28

I have seen that translated as a couple of bucks... can you appreciate the difference between, two dollars and two million dollars?

"He grabbed him and began to choke him, 'Pay back what you owe me! ' He demanded. His fellow servant fell to his knees and begged him, 'Be patient with me, and I will pay you back.' But he refused, instead, he went off and had the man thrown into prison until he could pay the debt. When the other servants saw what had happened, they

137

were greatly distressed and went and told their master everything that had happened. Then the master called the servant in, 'you wicked servant,' he said, 'I canceled all that debt of yours because you begged me to; shouldn't you have had mercy on your fellow servant just as I had on you?' In anger his master turned him over to the jailers to be tortured, until he should pay back all he owed."

Matthew 18:28-34

"Wow!" Did you see that? He not only had the servant thrown in jail, but he said they were to *torture* him every day until his debt was paid.

Now, I want you to look at the very next verse.

"This is how my heavenly Father will treat each of you unless you forgive your brother from your heart."

Matthew 18:35

Some people would say that we are to take that statement literally, while others would say we should take it figuratively. Here's a thought . . . *How about, we take it seriously?*

Well if it's that important - and it is - how are we to go about developing a forgiving heart?

CHAPTER THREE QUESTIONS

How many of the "things" that happen to us in our life can God use for our good? Give Scripture reference.

_____

_____

_____

_____

_____

Forgiveness deals with the response of our _____ toward our offender.

Pardon deals with the _____ of their offense.

Forgiveness involves a _____ attitude toward the offense, rather than a

_____ attitude toward the offender.

Discuss the statement: "What happens to us in life is not important."

_____

_____

_____

_____

_____

_____

_____

What character qualities does God want to develop in your life?

_____

_____

_____

_____

_____

_____

_____

_____

How would God help you to develop patience with people?

_____

_____

_____

_____

_____

Forgiveness views the offense as an _____ _____ in the hands of God. Give some examples from Scripture.

_____

_____

_____

_____

_____

_____

_____

_____

_____

Only God has the right to _____.
Give Scripture reference.

_____

_____

We understand this is God's instruction to individuals who might seek revenge
on someone who has wounded or offended
them. These are not instructions for those
in positions of God-ordained and delegated
authority.

Discuss how we should pray for our enemies.

_____

_____

_____

_____

_____

_____

_____

_____

Forgiveness involves _____
___ with God in the offender's life.

Discuss the story of the servant (Matt. 18:23-35).

_____

_____

_____

_____

_____

_____

_____

_____

_____

_____

_____

_____

CHAPTER FOUR

DEVELOPING A
FORGIVING HEART

He was the youngest of twelve sons. And he was daddy's favorite. Daddy even had a special coat made for him to identify him as the favorite son.

The rest of the boys all had to work while "Joey" laid around the house, "watching TV and playing video games."

One night Joey had a dream that his parents and brothers would work for him one day, and he was foolish enough to tell his brothers about his dream.

This only made his brothers hate and resent him more intensely than they already did. [This causes me to understand that, even if it were God that gave you a dream or a vision, it does not mean that you have to go around telling everybody about it. Sometimes we need to be like Mary and "ponder these things in our hearts."]

One day his father said, "I want you to go and check on your brothers and come and tell me what they're doing."

Joey went to check up on his brothers. They saw him coming and said, "Let's kill this dreamer and tell God he died."

No. What they really said was, "Let's kill this dreamer, throw his body in the well, dip his fancy coat in animal blood, and tell Dad that an animal killed him."

You know the story. Reuben had a streak of conscience and talked the other brothers out of killing him. "Let's just throw him in the pit," he insisted. The Bible says that he intended to come back and get Joey when the others were gone and take him home to their father.

However, while they were eating their lunch . . . (Can you imagine? They captured their brother, threw him in a pit, and casually sat down to eat their lunch.) Anyway, while they were eating their lunch, slave traders passed by on their way to Egypt and they sold Joey into slavery.

You remember that Joseph was placed in charge of Potiphar's household and Potiphar's wife made a move on him. Because of his integrity, however, Joseph refused to have sex with her. She cried "rape" and had him thrown in prison.

Even in prison, God prospered Joseph and a number of years later, after he had interpreted the dreams of the cupbearer and the baker, the cupbearer finally remembers him and tells Pharaoh about him.

In one day, Joseph went from being a prisoner to being Prime Minister of the most powerful nation on Earth at that time.

God knows where you are and He knows how to get you where He wants you.

Joseph interpreted Pharaoh's dream and the drought came just as he said it would. Because of the drought, his brothers came to Egypt to purchase grain and once the whole family was in Egypt, Joseph reveals himself to his brothers. The Bible says that their knees "smote" one upon the other.

"He's going to have us killed," they thought. *"He's going to sell us into slavery or he's going to throw us into prison."*

Why in the world, would they think that Joseph would do those things to them? Probably because that is what they did to him and they could not imagine someone forgiving them for what they had done.

But Joseph had seen God working through his brothers' actions and, in Genesis 50:20 (NIV), he says:

"You intended to harm me, but God intended it for good to accomplish what is now being done, the saving of many lives."

Look at Psalm 76:10:

"Surely the wrath of man shall praise thee; the remainder of wrath shalt thou restrain."

That's Romans 8:28 in the Old Testament!!!

By that I mean, this Old Testament verse teaches the same principal as Romans 8:28: *"And we know that all things work together for good . . ."*

God is saying that He can take even the wrath of man and turn it around and use it for His praise. He can even take the bad things that happen to us, turn them around, and use them for our good.

"The remainder of wrath shalt thou restrain." Do you know what that means? It

means if God cannot get praise from it, or if He cannot use it for our good, He will not allow it happen!

Joseph understood that God was working through the actions of his offenders. His brothers were simply the tools, which God used to accomplish what He wanted for Joseph's life.

Well glory! God *is* in control. We need to realize that God is working through the actions of our offenders.

1. So, step one in developing a forgiving heart is to realize that God is working **through the actions** of your offender.

As long as we think the one who hurt us was acting independently, we can hardly help but grow bitter.

2. Step two is that we can **thank him for the benefits** He plans through every offense that comes our way. Because whatever God allows, He can use to bring praise to His name; and He can use it for our good.

The Scripture tells us:

"In everything give thanks: for this is the will of God in Christ Jesus concerning you."

I Thessalonians 5:18

It does not say to give thanks "for" everything, but "in everything." We do not have to feel thankful in order to thank God. Giving thanks is like forgiveness; it is an act of our will. Feeling thankful is simply an act of our emotions.

When our lives are committed to God, and we are walking in obedience to Him, He puts a protective wall around us so that nothing can touch us except that which God permits.

What He permits, He permits for a purpose; and that purpose is for our ultimate joy and reward. It is for this reason we can thank God for every offense that comes our way.

3. The third step toward developing a forgiving heart is to figure out what character qualities God wants to develop in you, through the offense.

When you react wrongfully toward an offender, you are revealing various character deficits that need to be developed in you. Godly character traits such as:

Love, meekness, patience, faith, gentleness, self-control, etc.

As we said before, these are all character traits that God will help us to develop over the course of our lives.

4. The fourth step in developing a forgiving heart is simply to expect that to suffer for doing right, is a normal part of Christian living.

Many people have the mistaken idea that if they are a Christian, or if they just have enough faith, they will not have to suffer.

Did Jesus have faith?

The world misunderstood and persecuted Jesus. The Bible tells us He *"learned obedience by the things that He suffered."* What makes you think the world will not persecute you? Or what makes you think you will not have to suffer?

> *"For unto you it is given in the behalf of Christ, not only to believe on him, but also to suffer for his sake:"*
>
> Philippians 1:29

> *"Yea, and all that will live godly in Christ Jesus shall suffer persecution."*
>
> II Timothy 3:12

We must not think of this as a negative. For . . .

> *"If we suffer, we shall also reign with him."*
>
> II Timothy 2:12

We need to keep in mind that although it may be painful, and the wounds may hurt, the important thing is not what happens to us in life . . .

THE IMPORTANT THING IS HOW WE RESPOND TO WHAT HAPPENS TO US IN LIFE.

When we are humble, God gives us grace. When we respond with God's grace to life's hurts and wounds, then God is free to move in the hearts and lives of those around us.

That is what happened to Judy when she developed a forgiving heart. God moved in her entire extended family because she chose to forgive.

As a little girl, Judy rode the bus and attended Sunday school at the church in Twin

Falls, Idaho where Jim Hicks was the pastor. But as a teenager, Judy quit going to church, drifted away from God, got married, had a little girl, a little boy named Steve, and then went through a very tragic divorce.

Later, Judy married Lyle who, by his own testimony, had become a backslidden alcoholic. Together they had a little boy named Matthew. However, because of Lyle's drinking, their marriage was in trouble.

At that point, Steve was a senior in high school and had become a Christian because of the influence of his grandfather.

Jim Hicks had semi-retired by then, and was serving as the Christian education director on my ministerial staff (in the same church where he used to be the pastor).

My youngest son, Ron, and Pastor Hick's grandson were also seniors and, although

Ron did not go to school with Steve or pastor Hick's grandson, they all knew each other from common youth gatherings and Christian activities.

After graduation, Ron went to Bible school in the Northwest and Steve joined the Marine Corps.

After eight months of infantry and security forces training, Steve came home for thirty days leave on his way to his duty assignment in Iceland.

While he was home, Steve talked to his mother about the Lord. He mentioned that he was worried about being able to live a Christ-like life and set a Christian example in the atmosphere of the Marine Corps.

After talking and praying with his home-town pastor, Steve boarded a plane and flew to Iceland. He found his bunk in the barracks, arranged his footlocker, hung his clothes in the closet "Marine style," took a shower, changed into his duty uniform, then sat down on his bunk to write an entry in his journal.

In his journal entry, he wrote that it was his desire to be a witness and to be able to lead other Marines to a saving knowledge of Jesus Christ. He got up, put his journal in his footlocker, smoothed the bed, and reported to his duty station.

It had been less than eleven hours since the plane had touched down on the runway in Iceland.

As Steve walked through the door to his duty assignment, another Marine lowered a rifle at his head and said, "Shall I shoot you or shoot myself?" He then pulled the trigger and blew Steve into eternity!!!

Judy received a knock on the door in Jerome, Idaho. Opening the door, she saw two Marine officers. "Mrs. McClimans?"

"Yes."

"We're very sorry to tell you your son, Steve, has been killed."

Judy recounted, "I almost collapsed on the porch."

We have all heard stories of people turning their back on God and blaming Him when tragedy happens. With Judy, it was just the opposite. "I ran back to God as fast as I could. I knew I could not survive the pain, guilt, and eventual anger without the Lord," she told me.

Pastor Hicks heard about this tragedy right away since he lived in Jerome and his grandson had known Steve. He went to Lyle and Judy's house and prayed with them almost every day for several weeks. Lyle and Judy, their daughter, and two-year-old son Matthew, started attending our church.

Several months later, Judy asked if she and Lyle could meet with me in my office. We met on a Monday morning. They sat in front of my desk Lyle was extremely shy and quiet; he kept his head down and would not even look at me.

Judy said, "Pastor, we are going to make this our church home and we were wondering if you would dedicate our son, Matthew?"

I asked one of the most difficult questions I have ever asked anyone. "Judy," I asked, "have you come to the place in your heart where you have been able to forgive the young man who killed your son?"

I braced myself for her response. I was expecting a tirade of bitterness. I was shocked by what I heard, but it prepared the way for God's miraculous intervention in Judy's entire family.

"The day those officers came to tell us that Steve had been shot, my world stopped," She said. "It was indescribable pain, emotionally and physically. Seeing my son in a casket was the worst day of my life. *'God,'* I thought, *'how can I live with this?'*"

Steve was only 19 and someone had ripped his life away in one second. Judy discovered an anger and hatred she never knew she could feel.

"But within a month," she said, "we started coming back to church. That Sunday morning, my heart was so broken that I didn't know if it could be mended."

At the close of that service, I had invited people to come to the altar for prayer and Judy had come forward while we were singing *Because He Lives (I can face tomorrow)*.

Judy stood at the altar, weeping and crying out for peace, and God gave her that peace as she found herself praying for the man who had killed her son.

She knew absolutely nothing about the Marine, except that his name was Jon, he tried to commit suicide a couple days after the incident, and was under a 24-hour watch until the trial.

"I knew that as long as I had unforgiveness in my heart," she said, "I could not start the healing process. Then, I heard myself crying out to God, *'Please, God, don't let Jon die, too.'* It almost shocked me, I was praying for the man that had killed my son." What grace God had given her to be able to forgive!

Before the trial, Lyle and Judy stood outside the courtroom knowing that as soon as they entered they would come face-to-face with their son's killer. Judy prayed a quick prayer, asking God to give her strength and courage when she saw the young man.

If you were to ask any of the other Marines on the base about Jon, they would have said he was a very muscular and strong young man who worked out and lifted weights regularly. He was something of a "bully" who led the hazing of new arrivals on the base.

Judy said, "When I saw him, I was shocked to see a young man with a baby face, looking so scared and frightened because the rest of his life was in the hands of eight military officers."

The court determined that the shooting was not deliberate, but was a hazing incident gone too far. Jon was found guilty of manslaughter by culpable negligence.

Judy's testimony at the sentencing hearing would help determine the severity of his sentence. While she was on the stand, the prosecuting attorney asked her to describe her anger and hate toward the defendant.

"I feel no anger toward him, and I don't hate him," Judy said. "I have forgiven him."

After the sentencing, as they were taking Jon away, he asked if he could talk to Judy. She agreed.

They nearly collapsed in each other's arms; both of them sobbing almost uncontrollably. "Oh, Mrs. McClimans," Jon said, "If I could change places with Steve, I would."

Judy said, "Jon, if Steve could change places with you, he wouldn't do it. He is with his Lord - whom he loved and served."

It was amazing to see God's power released in Judy's family, because of her forgiving heart.

First her husband, Lyle, was saved and delivered from alcohol. Then her daughter was saved. Next, her daughter's fiancée was saved; and we later performed their wedding. Then, one-by-one, her three sisters came to know Jesus as their personal Savior. Her mother was saved and attended church for some time before she died; and her father, who had not been in a church for over fifty years, came to the altar and made a profession of faith.

Her brother-in-law, her nephews, and her uncle were all saved - because Judy decided to develop a forgiving heart.

Eventually, through her testimony and personal correspondence, Jon also came to know Jesus Christ as his Savior.

Salvation spread like ever-increasing ripples after a stone has been thrown into calm waters.

Jesus said:

"I tell you the truth, unless a kernel of wheat falls to the ground and dies, it remains only a single seed, but if it dies, it produces many seeds."

John 12:24 NIV

Can God bring good things out of tragedy? The answer is a glorious and resounding . . .

YES!

"And we know that all things work together for good . . ."

CHAPTER FOUR QUESTIONS

Discuss step one in developing a forgiving heart.

_____

_____

_____

_____

_____

_____

_____

_____

Discuss step two in developing a forgiving heart.

_____

_____

_____

_____

_____

_____

_____

_____

_____

Discuss step three in developing a forgiving heart.

_____

_____

_____

_____

_____

_____

_____

_____

Discuss step four in developing a forgiving heart.

_____

_____

_____

_____

_____

_____

_____

_____

When we respond with God's grace to the wounds of life, then God is _____ _____ to move in the lives of others around us.

Discuss the question, "Can God bring good things out of tragedy?"

_____

_____

_____

_____

_____

_____

_____

_____

_____

_____

_____

_____

_____

_____

Give examples from your own life.

_____

_____

_____

_____

_____

_____

_____

_____

_____

_____

_____

_____

_____

_____

_____

_____

CHAPTER FIVE

RESTORING
RELATIONSHIPS

While we were pastoring in Idaho, we had a somewhat strange occurrence. One Sunday, after the morning service, two different men came up and asked if they could meet with me in my office the following day. Both of these men were attending our church for the first time that day. Neither of them knew the other.

I told them, "Certainly, I will meet with you." I schedule the first man for a 10:00

a.m. appointment. When the second man approached and asked for an appointment, I scheduled him for 2:00 p.m.

The next morning, Don (not his real name), arrived for his appointment. After greeting him, I invited him to have a seat and asked what I could do for him.

"Pastor," he said, "I need your help. My wife left me Saturday and I don't know what to do."

"What do you mean, 'she left you'?" I asked.

He said, "I mean, she packed up and moved out of the house. She took everything she felt belonged to her: clothes, dishes, furniture . . . everything."

"How long have you been married?" I asked.

"Thirteen years," he said.

"And how long have you known there were problems in your marriage?" I asked.

"I didn't know there were any problems," he said.

"Well then, you must be dumber than a post," I said.

It's called shock therapy and it helps to cut through all the flack and get to the heart of the matter. After stuttering around for a minute or so, he finally admitted there had been problems for quite some time.

"How many of the problems would you say were your fault and how many were her fault?" I asked.

"Oh," he said, "about ten percent my fault and ninety percent her fault."

Since she wasn't there to defend herself, I let that go. "Well," I said, "let's concentrate on what you did that was wrong." I explained to him that if he would identify his wrong actions and attitudes and ask forgiveness for them, it would go a long ways toward restoring the relationship.

By the time I got him to identify his wrongs, he had it down to about one or two percent.

"It doesn't matter," I said. "When we go to someone to ask their forgiveness, we must only speak about what it was we did that was wrong. We have to leave their wrongs between them and God. He can convict their hearts just as He did ours."

That afternoon, Jim (not his real name), met me in my office.

"What can I do for you, Jim?" I asked.

"Pastor, I need your help. My wife left me Saturday and I don't know what to do." I swear those were his exact words!

I said, "What do you mean 'she left you'?"

He said (and I am not making this up), "She packed up and moved out of the house. She took everything she felt belonged to her and left. She took her clothes, the dishes, the furniture . . . everything."

"How long have you been married?" I asked.

"Eighteen years," he said.

"And how long have you known there were problems?" I asked.

"I didn't know there were problems," he said.

Really, I am not making this up! I could not believe that within the space of a couple of hours, two men I had never met (and who had never met each other), sat in my office and told me the same thing, almost word for word.

So I said to him, "If you have been married for eighteen years and you didn't know that there were problems until your wife moved out of the house, then you must be dumber than a post!"

*Why is it so hard for us, as men, to admit that we have a problem; or to seek help for the problems we have **before** the wife leaves the house?*

Is it because our society has taught us, since we were little boys, that we should not cry and that "real men" solve their own problems?

After Jim recovered from the shock of the pastor telling him he was "dumber than a post," he - like Don - finally admitted that there had been problems for years.

Also like Don, he said it was only ten percent his fault. Again, I think it must be something in a man's DNA that causes him to think the real problem is always with other people.

Why is it so hard for us to apologize or to admit that we are wrong?

Jesus dealt with this when He said:

"Why do you look at the speck of sawdust in your brother's eye and pay no attention to the plank in your own eye? How can you say to your brother, let me take the speck out of your eye, when all the time there is a plank in your own eye? You hypocrite, first take the plank out of your own eye, and then you will see clearly to remove the speck from your brother's eye."

Matthew 7:3-5 NIV

Paul was wrestling with the same basic problem when he wrote to Timothy. Then again, in the book of Acts, as he writes about "conscience."

"Timothy, my son, I give you this instruction in keeping with the prophecies once made about you, so that by following them you may fight the good fight, holding on to faith and a good conscience, some have rejected these and so have shipwrecked their faith."

I Timothy 1:18-19 NIV

"So I strive always to keep my conscience clear before God and man."

Acts 24:16 NIV

Having a clear conscience is not a high priority for some people. Paul says these people have *"shipwrecked their faith."*

I think the single greatest hindrance to seeking forgiveness from those we have offended, thereby clearing our conscience, is our feeling that the ones we hurt were also wrong.

In fact, like Jim and Don, we often feel that they were more wrong than we were. Our focus on blaming them seems to balance our own guilt and forces us to live with both guilt and blame.

When we are guilty of either wrong actions or wrong attitudes, we must either ask forgiveness or balance our guilt by blaming someone else. Our natural tendency is to blame other people or circumstances for what we have done, in order to justify or excuse *our* offenses.

I think it may be America's national pastime – to blame someone else!

I saw a t-shirt once that said, "I didn't say you did it, I just said I was going to blame you."

The greater our own guilt, the more we must blame others. The result is that the bitterness and guilt will devastate our mental and emotional well-being. But then, I've already covered that.

Before we ask forgiveness, let us look for a moment at the destructive power of *WRONG ATTITUDES*.

People react to our attitudes more than we realize. Therefore, it is essential that we learn how to "judge ourselves" in our wrong attitudes so that we will not be judged by others.

It is so important to confront, confess, and change our wrong attitudes; which were either caused by, or resulted from, our wrong actions.

This is a lot more difficult than we realize. We are so involved with our own thoughts and emotions that we fail to recognize the attitudes we are reflecting to the people around us.

Once, I heard a minister say, "We judge other people by what they do. We judge ourselves not by what we've done, but by what we *intended* to do."

I have spent several chapters talking about forgiving others. Now it is time to look at the other side of the coin.

What can we do when we were the ones that offended someone else? How do we go about asking them to forgive us? Should we go to them and ask them to forgive us?

CHAPTER FIVE QUESTIONS

What should we do if we are the one who has hurt another person?

_____

_____

_____

_____

_____

_____

_____

_____

What does Paul say will shipwreck our faith? Give Scripture reference.

_____

_____

_____

_____

What is our biggest hindrance to gaining a clear conscience?

_____

_____

_____

_____

_____

Discuss what you should do if the person you have offended was more wrong than you.

_____

_____

_____

_____

_____

_____

_____

CHAPTER SIX

RESOLVING CONFLICT

S o, how do we go about resolving conflict with a particular person?

I. The first step to resolving conflict with a particular person is to *privately list all the offenses* they committed against you.

Now, why would I say "privately"?

I say "privately" because of the teaching in Matthew, chapter 18. Jesus said if a person offended us we should go to that person "alone."

This is another verse that we don't believe or we just decide to ignore.

Instead of going "alone" to the person who offends us, we go and tell our spouse, or our friends. Or perhaps, if you're really "spiritual," you will go and tell your pastor.

The minute you go to someone other than the one who offended you, you have violated the teaching of Matthew 18.

I had a policy when I was a pastor. If someone came to me and asked, "Did you hear what so-and-so said about me?" I would not allow them to talk about it.

"No," I would say. "And I don't want to!"

When they would recover from the shock, they would usually ask, "Why?" And I would ask them whether they had gone to the individual and discussed it with him.

"No," they would say. "I was hoping you would go and talk with him."

"Well," I told them. "Jesus said that you were to go to him alone. If that doesn't work, take a friend or two with you. If that doesn't work, *then* you come and tell me and I will go."

If we would just learn to do what Jesus told us to do, we would limit the fallout and avoid many problems in our families and in the church.

So, privately make a list of all the party's offenses. Here are some common things that people do to offend us:

1. *Fail to keep their promises.* They never do what they say they are going to do.

2. *Blame us for things we did not do.* This is a common complaint teenagers have against their parents. Mom, dad . . . here's a tip: make sure they did it before you punish them.

3. *Say false things about us.* I had a lady come to me one time and say, "Pastor, sister so-and-so is going around town telling all kind of lies about me."

"Praise the Lord!" I said.

"What!" she said. "Why would you say that?"

"Well," I said, "praise the Lord, it's not the truth. How bad would it be if she was saying all kinds of terrible things about you and it was the truth?"

4. *Not understanding us.* If you are a husband, you might be saying, "Who understands women?"

Well, God says that you are supposed to. In I Peter 3:7, God says that we are to *"dwell with them according to knowledge . . . that your prayers be not hindered."*

Simply put, He is saying if we don't understand our wives, our prayers will be hindered. But, that's another book.

5. *Expect too much from us.* "Why do they always leave it for me to do?"

6. *Not there when we need them.* In the late 90's, I was invited to accompany Dave Reover the first time he led a group of 25 Vietnam veterans on a trip back to Vietnam.

When Dave asked me to bring the devotions on the last day we were to be in Saigon (now known as Ho Chi Mien City), I immediately felt the Lord wanted me to speak on the subject of "forgiveness."

All week I watched the veterans. Many of them were horribly wounded. Legs and arms blown off, burned by napalm, etc. I was expecting to see a lot of bitterness displayed. Instead, everyone seemed to be having a great time.

On Wednesday of that week, we had a meeting in the former Presidential Palace with 25 of the Viet Cong veterans.

We split them up into three groups, according to which part of the country they had been in. That, of course, meant our veterans were coming face-to-face with men against whom they had probably fought.

I thought, *"Oh! Oh! This has all the potential for fireworks."* Instead, after sharing one of their songs with us, the Viet Cong veterans asked our guys to share a song with them.

They taught them to sing *Amazing Grace* and *How Great Thou Art.*

After bringing the groups back together, we all had lunch and concluded the meeting with the entire group (our veterans and their veterans) singing, "Then sings my soul, my Savior God to thee . . . How great Thou art."

I watched the guys getting on the bus to return to the hotel. They were not walking; they were *floating* down the sidewalk to the buses - singing and joking and just having a great time.

I thought to myself, *"These guys aren't bitter. I'm not going to speak on the subject of forgiveness on Friday morning."*

Mentally I was leafing through my Bible trying to come up with something else to say when the Spirit of the Lord spoke to my heart and said, *"You teach what I told you to teach."*

"Well, yes Sir, I will." So, on Friday morning, I spoke on the subject of bitterness and forgiveness.

During the devotion, I mentioned that I had a series of six sermons on what I referred to as *The Cause and Cure of Bitterness*. I told them if any of them wanted the whole series they could give me their address and I would send them the tapes.

Twenty-two of the twenty-five men, and one of the pastors, asked for the tapes. I discovered that they were not bitter about what had happened in Vietnam; they were bitter about relationships back home.

When the pastor, I will call Tom, came to me and asked for the tapes, I asked if he wanted them so he could teach the series.

"No," he said. "I need to hear them. I'm eat up with bitterness."

"My goodness," I said. "What in the world happened?"

Tom explained that he had been the pastor of one of his denomination's largest churches and during the past few years had served as a national officer. "I was there for everybody," he said. "I was there for my congregation, my fellow ministers, and my fellow national officers. Then, about two years ago, my son was killed in an auto accident. And no one was there for me."

It is so easy for parents, ministers, teachers, etc., to be there for everyone else. Then, when they need help, they find themselves all alone.

7. How about this one: *Giving more love and attention to others than to me.*

One day, when our three boys were little, a well-meaning parishioner said to me, "Now Pastor, remember you are not to show favorites to your children. Make sure you treat them all alike."

May I say - that is the worst advice you can give a parent? If you treat children all alike, one will feel smothered and another will feel neglected.

Mom, Dad . . . your job is to discover the needs of each individual child and then meet those needs. I said "needs" not wants.

So, the first step in resolving conflict is to *privately* list all of their offenses.

II. Secondly, on the other side of the paper, make a list of all your offenses.

It's easy to remember others' faults; but when it comes to listing our own faults, we tend to get "sometimers." So, let us list some of the things that might apply.

1. <u>Poor Attitude</u>. If I were to ask those who know you, would they say you have a "good" attitude or a "bad" one?
2. <u>Ungratefulness</u>. When was the last time you thanked your boss for giving you a job; or your parents, for providing you with a home, food, and clothing?

One night, after services, a teenager said to me, "Pastor Britain, parents are supposed to provide a home, food, and clothing."

"I know," I said. "But some parents don't. If yours does, you should thank them."

3. <u>Stubbornness</u>. Would others say you are stubborn?

4. <u>Untruthfulness</u>. Have you, at times, told only part of the truth so others would agree with you?

Charles Finney, the great evangelist of the 19th century, defined lying by saying, "If you tell the truth with the intent of deceiving someone, you're lying."

By this definition, we don't have an honest politician in the country!

When our forefathers set up the judicial system, why do you think they required us to swear to "tell the truth, *the whole truth,* and nothing but the truth"?

5. <u>Bitterness</u>. Have you been harboring resentment and bitterness for things others have done toward you?

III. The third step in solving conflict is to ask forgiveness for the wrong things we have done.

This is by far the most difficult step to take. However, I have seen people who did it right, instantly restore relationships that had been broken for twenty years.

This step must be taken with an attitude of complete sincerity, humility, and genuine repentance.

In asking forgiveness, we need to first identify our basic offense. It will do little good to ask forgiveness for a small offense when, in reality, it is only a fraction of a much greater offense.

So, how do we go about it? Well, there are several ways to ask forgiveness which are guaranteed _not_ to work.

Just a few days before Christmas, I was in the computer and Internet center where several guys from our local church worked. Rodney (not his real name) asked me what I was doing now that I had moved back to Colorado.

When I told him I felt the Lord wanted me to teach a seminar on forgiveness and restoring relationships, he shared with me that he had just been married for three months and he was already in trouble.

"What do you mean?" I asked.

"Well," he said, "my wife and I had an argument and no matter what I do she won't make up."

I teasingly told him that after he had been married for a few years he would know he just needed to apologize.

"I tried that," he said. "It didn't work."

I asked him what he said.

"I went to her and said, 'If I offended you, or if I have done something wrong, I'm sorry.'"

"Well, no wonder that didn't work," I said. "That's not an apology, that's an accusation."

"What do you mean?" he asked.

I explained that when you go to someone and say, "If I have offended you, I'm sorry," what you are really saying is: **"I know you think I did something wrong, but I don't think I did."** Then people "throw gas on the fire" by saying something like, "I know I was wrong, but **you were too**."

"Then what should I do?" He asked.

"Well, there is a statement that reflects true sincerity and humility. You figure out what you did, either by your actions or by your attitude, and you say, **"God has convicted me of how wrong I was** (describe the wrong action or attitude). **I know I was wrong and I've come to ask if you will forgive me**."

A couple of months later, Rodney saw me come back into the computer store. He called out, "Pastor Britain. I did what you told me to do."

I froze. My mind was spinning. "What did I tell you to do?" I asked. I had forgotten all about the incident.

"I apologized to my wife, the way you told me to," he said.

"And what happened?" I asked.

"She just melted," he said.

If we want to restore the relationship, when we ask forgiveness we must only refer to what *we* did. Even if we believe what we did wrong was only a small fraction of the overall problem.

We must leave whatever they did between them and God. He can bring conviction in their heart just as He did to ours.

I had been out of high school for ten years before I went to Bible College. Arriving a week late for the winter semester, I met with my faculty adviser and arranged my schedule.

Although I had transferred a year's worth of credits from a state college, he tried to get me to take several freshman courses, which he said I would need for graduation.

Sensing the need to make up for wasted years, I told him I was not down there to graduate, but to get "Bible and theology and get started preaching."

Thus, I took all of my junior and senior Bible and theology courses during the first two years I was there. One thing led to another, time passed, and suddenly I was just a semester away from graduation. But I needed to take Philosophy 101.

Dr. Mullen (not his real name), from whom I had taken a number of Bible and Christian ministry courses, was to be the teacher.

That particular semester, Dr. Mullen was going to graduate school to get his Ph.D. He was teaching at the Bible College and he was the pastor of a church.

I had always gotten straight A's in Dr. Mullen's classes and I enjoyed his teaching. He never taught from the textbook. He always figured we could read the textbook; but, to make sure we did, the mid-term test covered the first half of the book and the final covered the last half of the book. It was the same in all his classes.

In addition to the two tests, he would assign anywhere from one to four term papers (depending on the class); and, together with the tests, they made up our semester grade. I had received an "A" on all the papers I had ever written for Dr. Mullen.

Everything seemed to be going routinely. I got an "A" on the mid-term. Then, as term papers were coming due, Dr. Mullen would assign a student to read his paper and then he would not show up for class.

That ticked me off!

Every time a student was assigned a date to read his paper, Dr. Mullen would not be in class. I don't know why. But the more it happened, the angrier I became.

I violated Matthew 18 and I didn't go to him and talk with him about it. Instead, I told my friends how angry I was. *"I know what I'll do,"* I thought.

"I'll show him!"

"I won't write a paper!"

And I got an "F" on my term paper.

"Boy! I showed him!"

As the semester continued, the pattern of his absence continued and I got more and more angry. By now, the mere mention of his name made me so angry the veins on my neck would stand out.

"If he's not interested in teaching this class," I thought, "then I'm not going to study for the final."

So I didn't.

And I got an "F" on the final.

"I guess I showed him!!!"

I don't know if it was because he knew me and I had always done well in his classes, or if he just had mercy on me, but instead of flunking me or giving me an incomplete, he gave me a "D" for the course.

That "D" almost kept me from being accepted into graduate school.

"I guess I showed him."

Five years after graduation, I was the pastor of a church in Southeast Colorado. Every year, in January, our District would have a minister's meeting and bring in special speakers to preach and teach seminars. I loved going to those meetings!

One day, I received a phone call from our Superintendent; he was coming through our town and wanted to invite me to have coffee.

"Ted," he said, "I've got good news."

Excited, I asked, "What?"

"A friend of yours is going to be the speaker at the Minister's Institute," he said.

"Who?" I asked, eager to hear which of my friends it would be.

"Dr. Mullen," he said.

"Oooh," I said, trying to hide my disappointment.

I went home and told my wife that we would not be going to the Institute that year because we could not afford it.

I had not only violated Matthew 18, but now I was lying. It did not cost us anything to go to the Minister's Institute; our church always paid our expenses.

I sensed in my spirit that God was not happy with my bitterness, so I prayed and said, "Lord I forgive Dr. Mullen." I got up from my place of prayer feeling much better.

"Honey," I said, "I guess we can go to the Minister's Institute after all."

We had just registered and were walking across the campus of the old Denver campgrounds when a car pulled into the circular driveway. The back window rolled down and Dr. Mullen leaned out, waved, and shouted across the campus, "Hi, Ted."

I waved back, "Hi, Doc," I shouted cheer-fully. But as I turned to go to my car I felt a surge of anger rising up within me and I thought, *"You old reprobate!!"*

The anger was so powerful it shocked me. I thought I had taken care of it.

We returned to the motel and I prayed until service time. *"Lord, I'm so sorry, please forgive me of my bitterness, and I forgive Dr. Mullen for not being in class."*

I felt better.

We went to the service that night and Dr Mullen taught. He said, "Pastors, don't get so busy with the ministry that you neglect your family."

I thought, *"Yea, that's exactly what you did. You not only neglected your family, you neglected your students,"* and the anger was back in full force.

I know now why they call them "rednecks." When you get that angry, your veins stick out and your neck gets red.

After the service, we went back to the motel and I prayed until almost two in the morning. *"Lord forgive me. Lord, please take this bitterness out of my heart."*

And in my spirit I heard the Lord say, *"Do you really want to be free from your bitterness?"*

"Yes, Lord, I do."

"Then tomorrow morning you go to Dr. Mullen and apologize to him and ask him to forgive you."

*"**I will not!**"* I said emphatically.

"Why should I apologize, I'm not the one that skipped classes?"

If you give God half a chance, He will speak to you in very plain language, and it will

213

not be in "Elizabethan, King James English." What I heard was:

"You need to apologize for your rotten, stinking attitude, and for violating Matthew 18."

Up to this point I had never talked to Dr. Mullen about this; he didn't even know that I was upset with him.

Finally, at two in the morning I surrendered my will and said that I would apologize, but the devil kept telling me, *"It wouldn't do any good."*

After the morning service, I waited until others were done talking to him and then I approached him.

"Dr. Mullen," I said, "during my last semester in school, I got upset at you and said some unkind things about you to some of my friends. I want to tell you that God has convicted me of how wrong I was. I have come to ask, will you forgive me?"

He threw his arms around me, gave me a big hug, and said, "Of course, Ted, I forgive you."

Our relationship was instantly restored. That was over thirty years ago and I have never felt anger toward him since.

Several times through the years, I had Dr. Mullen speak in the churches where I was the pastor. We also helped him with the costs of some of his mission trips, when he taught overseas during the summers.

The last time I saw him, I took him out and bought him a big steak dinner and we talked about "the good ole days" for several hours. I have considered him a good friend over the years.

"That's all well and good," you say, "but why should I dig up the past and try to make things right?"

Because Jesus said:

"I say unto you, that whosoever is angry with his brother without a cause shall be in danger of the judgment; and whosoever shall say to his brother, Raca, shall be in danger of the council; but whosoever shall say, thou fool, shall be in danger of hell fire, therefore if thou bring thy gift to the altar, and there rememberest that thy brother hath ought against thee, leave there thy gift before the altar, and go thy way; first be reconciled to thy brother, and then come and offer thy gift."

Matthew 5:22-24

I am sure that anyone who has ever had the experience of making things right will remember the many reasons they had for *not* asking forgiveness.

Let's look at a few of the common rationalizations:

1. *It happened a long time ago.* So why is it still bothering you?
2. *The one I wronged has moved away.* With all the friends they left behind, I am sure you could find out where they are.
3. *It was such a small offense.* I am sure you think it was small; but again, if it was such a small offense, why is it bothering you?
4. *I am just being too sensitive.* So is the one you offended. A sensitive nature is

not something from which to shy away. Rather, it is something you should try to develop.

In Hebrews 5:14, Paul said, *"Strong meat belongeth to them that are of full age, even those who by reason of use have their senses exercised to discern both good and evil."*

5. *No one is perfect.* That is true. But apparently your standard of perfection is too low.

6. *They are not Christians. What will they think?* That is the excuse I used to avoid going to my father.

CHAPTER SIX QUESTIONS

Discuss the first step in resolving conflict.

_____

_____

_____

_____

_____

_____

_____

_____

Discuss the second step in resolving conflict.

_____

_____

_____

_____

_____

_____

_____

_____

_____

_____

Discuss the third step in resolving conflict.

_____

_____

_____

_____

_____

_____

When we ask forgiveness, what are some things we should <u>not</u> say?

_____

_____

_____

_____

_____

What should we say?

_____

_____

_____

_____

_____

_____

_____

What should our attitude be when we ask someone to forgive us?

_____

_____

_____

_____

_____

Why should we "dig up the past" and make things right?

_____

_____

_____

_____

_____

_____

_____

_____

_____

What excuses have you used to keep from asking others to forgive you?

_____

_____

_____

_____

_____

_____

_____

_____

_____

_____

CHAPTER SEVEN

MY DAD

We were concluding two weeks of revival services with evangelist Bill Hays. As he closed the service he had us stand and bow our heads and said, "I'm going to pray, and if there is someone you need to go to and ask them to forgive you, I am going to ask the Lord to bring their name to the forefront of your mind."

"Well," I thought. "I'm home free on this one." It had been about six months since I had gone to Dr. Mullen and asked him for his forgiveness. As far as I knew, there wasn't anyone else I needed to ask to forgive me.

However, as soon as Bill started to pray, God forcefully - in living color - brought an image of my father's face before my mind.

"Lord?" I asked. *"Why am I thinking about my dad?"*

"You need to go to him and ask him to forgive you," He said.

"For what?!" I asked.

"For being rebellious toward him while you were growing up," He replied.

Up to that very moment if you had asked me if I had ever been rebellious toward my dad, I would have said. "Are you kidding? If I had been rebellious, my dad wouldn't have allowed me to live."

I need to tell you a few things about my dad. First, he was not a Christian. Oh, he was a good man; very moral and hard working. He did not drink and I don't remember my mother and father ever arguing or raising their voices to one another.

Nor do I remember him ever hugging me, or telling me he loved me. I knew he did, but my dad was just not one to verbalize those kinds of emotions.

My dad never went to church with us. Not even on Easter or Christmas. And he never let me talk to him about God. If I even mentioned the words church, Bible, Jesus, God, or anything remotely religious, he would cut me off at the knees. "Don't you talk to me about God," he would say.

I used to pray, *"Lord soften my dad's heart."* I thought he was just "hard" toward God.

Now God was saying that I had been rebellious toward my father while I was growing up.

"Lord," I said, *"I wasn't rebellious toward my father."*

"Yes, you were." He said. And then He showed me what rebellion was.

I had a flashback to when I was in Junior High. I was sitting in the living room reading and my dad came in and asked me to go mow the lawn.

"Okay, Dad. I will."

He left and I kept on reading. About an hour later, he came back into the room and told me again to mow the lawn.

"Okay, Dad."

A half hour later, when he came back into the room, he was reaching for his leather belt, and I got up with great haste, and went to "mow the lawn."

As I was leaving the room I heard my dad say, "I never had to ask your brother twice."

My brother was ten years older than I was; and I had always looked up to him, and idolized him.

I had never thought of that incident before, but now the Lord was bringing it back to my memory and He said, *"If the one who has authority over you has to <u>make</u> you do what they ask you to do, then you're rebellious."*

"Oh Lord, forgive me." I suddenly realized that when I was a boy living at home, my father often had to "make" me do what he wanted me to do.

That night, I told my wife I needed to take a trip to South Dakota and see my Dad. So the next morning, I left our only car with my wife and three small sons, and I took a Greyhound bus from Rocky Ford, Colorado to Hot Springs, South Dakota.

My dad had been in and out of the hospital with heart problems for ten years and he just happened to be in the V.A. hospital when I arrived, after a day and a half of traveling by bus.

I got off the bus and took a taxi to the hospital and found my father's ward. Sitting beside his bed, we exchanged greetings. For him that meant a handshake, and then we visited for a while. Finally, I said, "Dad, I need to tell you something. God has convicted me of how rebellious I was toward you while I was growing up, would you forgive me?"

For the first time in my life, I saw tears flowing down his cheeks. He leaned forward, grabbed hold of me, drew me to himself, and held me in a tight hug as he was weeping, and said, "Son, I forgive you and I love you."

Instantly, our relationship, which I had always thought was good, was now great.

I did not know, until that day, that my dad had always thought of me as his rebellious son, but God knew.

I left the hospital with a light heart and spent the night with my mother. The next day the doctors released dad, so I used his car and took him home.

That night, I sat at my father's kitchen table and for two and a half hours he allowed me to talk to him about Jesus. I had thought he was hard toward God. Turns out, he just was not about to let a son he thought of as "rebellious" tell him about God.

About six months later, my dad went to the veterans' hospital in Denver, Colorado to undergo quadruple by-pass surgery. Two days after the surgery, while he was in intensive care, he had a massive heart attack.

The doctors told us he was not going to make it and allowed us to see him for only five minutes every hour.

During one of those visits, I told him I had to go home for some business and I would be back in about six hours.

"Don't leave me," he said.

Taking his hand, I said, "Dad, can I pray for you?"

"Yes," he said.

And there in the intensive care center, I led my Dad in the sinner's prayer. That night He stepped into eternity.

I don't think my dad would ever have allowed me to pray with him if I had not asked for his forgiveness. Since that time,

I have often wondered how many people turn down our invitation to "go to church," because they are remembering some offense from the past and we have never asked them for forgiveness; and they don't want to go to church with someone they consider to be a "hypocrite."

As I close this chapter, I want to pray for you, the reader.

Father, we desire to give you glory in our lives. We know we cannot do that if we have unresolved conflict with others. So I pray that if those who are reading these words need to go to someone and "make it right," and ask forgiveness, that you would bring the name of that person to their mind. And Father, I pray that you would give

*them the courage to go, and the words
to speak, to resolve the conflict and to
restore the relationship.*

*"We ask this in the name of your
strong Son, Jesus. Amen!"*

Allow me to add a short P.S.

About once every two weeks or so,
someone asks me, "What should you do if the
person you need to apologize to has already
passed away?" That's a good question. I tell
them they should go to someone that knew
them both and say, "If _____
were here now, I would say to them, 'God
has convicted me of how wrong I was. Would
you forgive me?'"

Healing in our hearts occurs when we
confess our wrongs to others.

"Therefore confess your sins to each other and pray for each other so that you may be healed."

James 5:16 NIV

CHAPTER SEVEN QUESTIONS

Has the Lord brought someone to mind that you need to go to and ask for forgiveness?

_____

_____

_____

_____

How would you go about doing it?

_____

_____

_____

_____

_____

_____

A WORD OF ENCOURAGEMENT

If the Lord has asked you to go to someone and ask for their forgiveness, He has already been working on them as well. If they should respond to you in a negative way, then you have done what the Lord has asked you to do and He will release your spirit of the burden.

Do not turn the meeting into a confrontation and accuse them of wrongdoing. Let them know that you care for them and excuse yourself. At this point God will deal with them. Leave them in His capable hands (Rom. 12:17-20).

Discuss whether God is able.

_____

_____

_____

_____

_____

_____

_____

_____

Discuss whether you agree with this author on the definition of *rebellion*.

_____

_____

_____

_____

_____

_____

_____

_____

_____